Criminal Enforcement of Environmental Law in the European Union

Comparative Environmental Law & Policy Series

VOLUME 8

The aim of the Editors and the Editorial Board of this series is to publish works of excellent quality that focus on the comparative study of environmental law and policy of countries of groups of countries.

Through the comparative study of environmental law and policy, the Editors and the Editorial Board hope:

- to contribute to the improvement of the quality of environmental law and policy in general and environmental quality in particular;
- to increase the access to environmental information and environmental justice for students, academics, non-governmental organizations, government institutions, and business;
- to facilitate cooperation between academic and non-academic communities in the field of environmental law and policy throughout the world.

Criminal Enforcement of Environmental Law in the European Union

edited by

Michael Faure

Maastricht European Institute for Transnational Legal Research, The Netherlands

and

Günter Heine

Institute for Criminal Law and Criminology, University of Berne, Switzerland

KLUWER LAW

INTERNATIONAL

A C.I.P. catalogue record for this book is available from the Library of Congress.

ISBN 90-411-2337-7

Published by:
Kluwer Law International
P.O. Box 85889
2508 CN The Hague
The Netherlands

Sold and distributed in North, Central and South America by:
Aspen Publishers, Inc.
7201 McKinney Circle
Frederick, MD 21704
USA

Sold and distributed in all other countries by:
Turpin Distribution Services Ltd.
Stratton Business Park
Pegasus Drive
Biggleswade
Bedfordshire SG18 8TQ
United Kingdom

Printed on acid-free paper

Printed in the Netherlands

CONTENTS

INTRODUCTION

The IMPEL Working Group on Criminal Prosecution has commissioned METRO to draft a report in order to provide the members of the working group with an insight into the systems and methods of criminal prosecution in environmental cases in practice. The idea is that this insight into the experiences in the various Member States will benefit all.

This report and research project is also a follow-up to an earlier project performed by METRO at the request of the Dutch public ministry, which participates in the IMPEL network. In 1997, METRO drafted a report called *Environmental Criminal Law in the European Union*, which provided an introduction to the environmental legal system in the Member States of the European Union, especially as far as the role of criminal law is concerned. That report provided a brief overview of the most important provisions concerning environmental law and the basic legislative framework that is used to apply environmental criminal law.[1] The current research project goes one step further in that it aims at providing a basic insight into the criminal enforcement in practice in each of the Member States. Whereas the first report focused on theory, this project is more concerned with the practice of environmental criminal law enforcement. This obviously has consequences for the methodology chosen.

This report is based on a comprehensive questionnaire related to specific topics concerning environmental criminal law, which has been made up by

---

[1] The results of that first report were published in Faure, M. and Heine, G., *Environmental Criminal Law in the European Union. Documentation of the main provisions with introductions*, Freiburg im Breisgau, Max Planck Institut for foreign and international criminal law, 2000.

the IMPEL ad hoc working group on criminal prosecution in environmental cases. On the basis of this questionnaire, country reports have been provided by the following Member States: Austria, Belgium, Denmark, Finland, Germany, Italy, The Netherlands, Portugal, Spain and the United Kingdom. As far as the United Kingdom is concerned we should point to the difficulty that different legal systems are involved, these being England and Wales on the one hand and Scotland on the other hand. The responses given relate only to the situation in England and Wales. In addition, some information was provided by the representative of Sweden, although this information does not provide answers to the questionnaire. Moreover, after the report was finished, Professor Marcel Bayle was asked to provide the answers for France as well since the editors judged that the information with respect to France should be included in this report.

The current volume is hence principally made up of the country reports drafted on the basis of the questionnaire. Therefore, both the questionnaire and the various country reports are included in the annexes to this report.

The goal of the comparative report presented in this volume is on the one hand to provide a summary of the various answers and to address differences and similarities in the practice with respect to environmental criminal law in the various countries, and on the other, it is to evaluate critically these answers. Hence, a summary of the various answers will be provided in II, whereas in the following chapter (III) a more evaluative analysis of these answers will be given. That evaluation will be made by using comparative law and addressing international tendencies. In that respect, attention will especially be given to the Council of Europe draft convention for the protection of the environment through criminal law[2] and the resolutions adopted at the XVth international congress of penal law (Rio de Janeiro, 4–10 September 1994).[3] Although we shall only focus on the Council of Europe Convention and the AIDP resolutions, the reader should be aware of the fact that a number of other organizations have taken action with respect to criminal environmental law as well.

In this respect, it is possible, for instance, to refer to various initiatives which were taken within the UN framework, such as Resolution 1993/28 of 27 July 1993 of the Economic and Social Council on the role of the criminal

---

2 Published in Van den Wyngaert, Ch. and Stessens, G. (eds.), *International Criminal Law. A Collection of International and European Instruments*, The Hague, Kluwer Law International, 1996, 135–141. See on the earlier Council of Europe Resolution concerning the use of criminal law for the protection of the environment also Vercher, A., 'The Use of Criminal Law for the Protection of the Environment in Europe: Council of Europe Resolution (77) 28', *Northwestern Journal of Internal Law and Business*, 1990, 442–459.

3 *International Review of Penal Law*, 1994, 47–53.

law in the protection of the environment. These documents are, however, less specific than the Council of Europe Convention and the AIDP resolutions; therefore we shall focus on those. Moreover, since the first draft of the report was finished, a number of changes have taken place at the European level. More particularly the European Commission launched the initiative for a proposal for a Directive on the Protection of the Environment through Criminal Law in 2001,[4] and on 27 January 2003 the Council adopted a resolution on the same theme. At this moment, the status of these documents is uncertain since the Commission has challenged the legality of the Council resolution before the European Court of Justice.[5] The Council resolution almost literally copied the Council of Europe Convention, which again justifies a brief look at this Council of Europe Convention since it provides interesting insights on how environmental criminal law should be structured.

Obviously, the reader should be aware of the fact that an elaborate legal doctrine has developed with respect to environmental criminal law, which can of course not be considered within the scope of this report. Some of this literature is, however, addressed in the list of references.

This report is drafted by Michael Faure and Günter Heine. Michael Faure is academic director of METRO and professor of comparative and international environmental law at the law faculty of Maastricht University. Günter Heine is professor of criminal law at the law faculty of the University of Berne and coordinator of the project 'Umweltschutz durch Strafrecht?' at the Freiburger Max Planck Institute for Foreign and International Criminal Law.

As far as the working method is concerned, we should mention that a first draft was provided to the members of the ad hoc working group on prosecution by 1 April 1998. This first draft was discussed in Helsinki in the presence of Günther Heine on 20–21 April 1998. All comments made during these discussions and the comments received in writing after the meeting have been incorporated. We are grateful to all those who contributed to this report by providing us comments on the earlier draft.

As far as the methodology is concerned, we should also mention that as far as possible we have attempted to provide in part II an objective summary of the facts as stated in the country reports. In some cases, we provided missing information ourselves. In part III, where the normative analysis is provided, this analysis is based on legal doctrine as well as on opinions in legal writing.

---

4 COM (2001) 139 final.

5 See on this conflict of competences Comte-Horeanga, F., 'Criminal Environmental Law and Community Competence', *European Environmental Law Review*, 2003, 147–156.

After the report was first concluded the reporters were asked to update the information originally provided and to bring it to the state of 2003. Moreover, a report on the situation in France was added. Hence, most, although not all, national reports reflect the situation up to 2003; we have subsequently also updated the summary of the country reports and the normative analysis. In the normative analysis recent evolutions, such as, for example, the initiatives at the European level, were obviously taken into account.

This study is set up as follows: After this introduction (I), a summary of the answers to the questionnaire is provided (II) followed by a critical analysis of the answers to each separate question (III). This report concludes with a few remarks (IV) and includes a few annexes. These annexes comprise obviously the questionnaire (annex 1), the country reports (annex 2), the Convention of the Council of Europe on the Protection of the Environment through Criminal Law (annex 3) and the resolutions of the AIDP conference on environmental criminal law (annex 4).

We are of course grateful to the country reporters for providing adequate and prompt responses to the questionnaire and to the IMPEL secretariat for its co-operation. Moreover, we are grateful to Anke Huijboom for useful research assistance and to Marina Jodogne for secretarial support.

Michael Faure and Günter Heine
Maastricht-Berne, October 2003

LIST OF CONTRIBUTORS

M. Christensen	Denmark
M. Faure	Maastricht University
A.M. Gepts	Belgium
G. Heine	University of Berne
V. Ljung	Sweden
B. Marshall	United Kingdom
E. Meyer-Rutz	Germany
A. Naves	Spain
M. Nissinen	Finland
P. Portugal	Portugal
M. Scaramella	Italy
P. Smutny	Austria
M.H. de Weert	The Netherlands

SUMMARY OF COUNTRY REPORTS

1. CRIMINAL LIABILITY OF CORPORATIONS FOR ENVIRONMENTAL OFFENCES

The questions deal with corporate criminal liability and the responsibility of directors and/or managers. Further consideration is given to the construction of corporate liability in practice.[1] Special attention is given to the problem of whether a legal person can be criminally liable in respect of the criminal responsibility of an individual person. In legal systems without corporate criminal liability, other ways of sanctioning companies are examined. In this case potential drawbacks should be explained. Table 1 categorizes these questions in five sections: corporate liability, prerequisites, other possibilities of sanctioning legal persons, drawbacks and, finally, liability of directors and/or managers.

First, the results of corporate criminal liability and its prerequisites are documented (in A), then other possibilities and drawbacks are considered (in B) and, finally, liability of directors/managers is discussed (in C).

1.1 Corporate liability

Denmark, France, Finland, the Netherlands, the United Kingdom and, since 1999, also Belgium are familiar with criminal liability of corporations, some of them have been for many years (United Kingdom, Netherlands since 1976),

---

1 These questions can be found in no. 1 of the questionnaire, Annex 1, pp. 99–101 of this volume.

Table 1. Criminal liability of corporations

Country	Corporate liability	Prerequisites	Other possibilities	Drawbacks	Liability of Directors
Austria	no corporate criminal liability		Confiscation, special provisions for legal persons in Penal Code	—	(+) – special provision in Administrative Penal code – Possibility of imposing liability on a person – Reversal of the burden of proof
Belgium	corporate criminal liability	– exclusion of public authorities – corporate? under specific conditions	– civil liability for fines – ban on exploiting the establishment over a period of time – confiscation of proceeds – administrative fines	limited possibility of liability of employees is debated	(+) cumulation is possible if the employee acted knowingly.
Denmark	yes	(−)	(−)	(+)	(+)
Finland	(+); ch. 9 sect. 1–9 P.C., ch. 48 sect. 9 (−); when crimes committed in the exercise of public authority	– guilt of a person of the managerial level – defective corporate organization, therefore corporate liability if employee committed crime, (guilty or not) – individual remains unidentified	(−)	(−)	(+)

Continued

Table 1. *Continued*

Country	Corporate liability	Prerequisites	Other possibilities	Drawbacks	Liability of Directors
France	Yes	Only liability for offences when the text indicates that liability is possible	(–)	– not applied to offences by the French State – not general for local public authorities	(+)
Germany	no corporate criminal liability	(–)	● corporate non-criminal fine (OwiG) ● contravention/crime of leading representatives ● violation of supervisory duties ● even in the case of non-identifying an individual when the crime as such can be contributed to a group of individuals* ● confiscation of illegal proceeds	● corporate criminal liability in political discussion* ● limited enforcement of corporate non-criminal fine	(+)
Italy	no corporate criminal liability	(–)	● fiscal, financial fines ● suspension of activities ● compensation ● restoration	● penalties imposed on individuals are too low	(+) all legal representatives, or responsibility for certain duties ● specific due diligence of representatives ● liability of delegates

Continued

Table 1 *Continued*

Country	Corporate liability	Prerequisites	Other possibilities	Drawbacks	Liability of Directors
The Netherlands	Yes	● corporate criminal liability if corporation normally accepts risky behaviour of the employee	—	—	(+) ● all managerial agents ● all employees
Portugal	no corporate criminal liability in respect of environmental crimes	(−)	● corporate non-criminal fine (OwiG)	?	(+)
Spain	no corporate criminal liability	(−)	—		(+) ● executives of company ● failure to meet the provided conditions
Sweden	no criminal liability, but corporate fine	● imposed on legal and physical persons ● crime with gross violation of entrepreneurial duties ● side sanction*	● environmental fee* ● independent of guilty behaviour* ● violation of the law and benefit to the company*		(+)
England and Wales	(+) case law	– organs; identification theory – employees: vicarious liability – environmental offences = strict liability offences; violation of supervisory duties – within the ordinary course of their business activities	—	—	(+)

Finland has enforced corporate criminal liability since 1995. As for historical reasons the traditional model of corporate criminal liability follows the identification theory, a key problem is the identification of an individual person imputing his fault (behaviour, personal guilt) to the corporation. However, the Member States are relaxing this traditional requirement: In Denmark, England and Wales liability is imposed on the enterprise irrespective of the guilt of an employee – what is decisive is the liability of the legal person itself. The principle in Denmark remains that the enterprise is liable if a person/employee is liable. But anonymous failures also result in corporate liability. On the one hand, Finland follows the classical identification theory (guilt of a person at the managerial level) while on the other hand corporate criminal liability occurs in the case of a defective corporate organization, which means that there is no need to identify a natural person as the actor. And in the Netherlands, whether corporations normally accept risky behaviour of the employee is the decisive point. Environmental offences are offences of strict liability, that is, no fault needs to be proved. For some environmental offences there is a due diligence defence which means that the company took all due diligence to avoid committing the offence. In Belgium legal entities are held liable for criminal offences which are 'intrinsically related to the realization of its aim or the representation of its interests, or which, as shown by concrete circumstances, have been committed on its behalf'. In Belgium it is hence not necessary to identify the physical person that would have committed an offence in order to hold the legal entity liable.[2]

1.2 Other possibilities and drawbacks

The other countries adhere to the principle *'societas delinquere non potest'*. However, some of them have established distinct forms of sanctioning enterprises. In 1987, Austria included a special provision in its penal code for legal persons confiscating illegal profits. And in Germany confiscating the proceeds of legal entities is possible under the penal code. Sweden as well does not accept a specific criminal liability of corporations but imposing a corporate fine, defined as a side sanction, is possible. This corporate fine can be imposed on legal and physical persons in the case of a crime with gross violation of entrepreneurial duties.

---

2 On the situation in Belgium in addition to the Belgian country report see also Faure, M., 'Criminal responsibilities of legal and collective entities: developments in Belgium', in Eser, A., Heine, G. and Huber, B. (eds.), *Criminal responsibility of legal and collective entities*, International Colloquium Berlin 1998, Max Planck Institute for foreign and international criminal law, Freiburg im Breisgau, 1999, 105–112.

Besides these possibilities, other measures do exist in many countries: for many years, Germany, Portugal and Italy have had a separate system in the administrative sphere: a kind of administrative penal law (Ordnungswidrigkeitenrecht). The Ordnungswidrigkeitengesetz provides a non-criminal fine that can be imposed on legal persons (Germany, Portugal). In Germany the maximum corporate fine is DM 1 million. Combined with seizure of illegal benefits the fine can amount to several million Deutsch Mark.[3] This corporate fine will be imposed in cases of administrative and criminal offences including violation of supervisory duties. It is no condition that an individual person of the enterprise is convicted if the offence as such can be attributed to a group of leading representatives. The Italian legislator allows a broad spectrum of sanctions against enterprises; fiscal and financial fines, suspension of activities, compensation and restoration, all of them legally regarded as non-criminal sanctions. And in Belgium a corporation can be held civilly liable for fines, even before the introduction of the criminal liability of the corporation. Confiscation of proceeds is also possible.

In 1987, Sweden established a new kind of sanction: a kind of environmental fee can be imposed on both legal and natural persons. This environmental fee is independent of guilty behaviour. The only conditions are the violation of an administrative regulation and benefit to the company.

Only some drawbacks are mentioned in the questionnaires: in Italy, it is a well-known problem that penalties imposed on individuals are too low. In Germany, in contrast to other fields, such as anti-trust law, there is only limited enforcement of corporate fines in the sphere of environmental protection.

1.3 Criminal liability of directors/managers

In all countries there exists criminal liability of directors and managers, although the conditions for imposing criminal liability are mostly not mentioned. However, in Denmark board members are charged when they acted either wilfully or by gross negligence, yet the priority is the company. In the Netherlands all material agents and all employees are criminally liable, while in Spain it is the company's executives. Italy differentiates between legal representatives and persons who have been delegated specific duties. There is a specific due diligence clause for representatives. Other countries, such as Austria and Germany, provide different sanctions between the personal criminal responsibility under the penal code and the personal liability under the

[3] The fines are further discussed in § 3 and § 4.

Ordnungswidrigkeitengesetz. As a rule the liability under the administrative penal law is broader than that of the criminal code. For example Germany has a special provision for the violation of supervisory duties. In Austria there is the possibility of appointing a person who will be held criminally liable in the enterprise under the administrative penal code. The appointed person can be held liable if he or she has agreed to the delegation of responsibility and is authorized to give instructions within the scope of his or her responsibility. If this person has caused a contravention in following an instruction of a person in a higher position, he or she cannot be held liable if there have been reasonable grounds for not complying with the law. In the Austrian administrative penal code it is not the duty of the authorities to prove liability of the actor. This is remarkable in so far as the burden of proof is reversed. Note also that in 2000, France changed the criminal liability of directors. As a result of the amendment, managers are exonerated when their imprudence or carelessness is only an indirect cause of the offence.

2. THE ROLE OF ENFORCING BODIES AND INDIVIDUALS IN CONNECTION WITH ENVIRONMENTAL OFFENCES

The various questions under Part 2 relate to the important issueregarding the role individuals (victims or NGOs) might play in criminal prosecutions. The same question is also raised with respect to environmental agencies, also referred to as enforcing bodies. The various questions more specifically relate to the relationship between individuals, enforcing bodies and the public prosecutor. All of the questions asked moreover relate to the role of police, individuals and enforcing bodies with respect to the prosecution of environmental cases before a criminal court. It is stressed (see questions 2(g) and (h)) that enforcing bodies can obviously play an important role with respect to the investigation and handling of administrative offences; in addition, individuals may play an important role, for instance when claiming compensation for environmental damage. However, the questions posed in 2(a) to (f) more particularly relate to the specific role of individuals and enforcing bodies in environmental criminal prosecutions.

In this respect, it must be mentioned that there might be a small linguistic problem which could lead to confusion. The term 'enforcing bodies' was used in the questionnaire since this was the expression used in the questionnaire provided to us. Apparently, this notion covers both administrative agencies that, for instance, issue permits (and are not necessarily involved in enforcement tasks) as well as administrative enforcement agencies which can for instance control or investigate and sometimes even impose administrative sanctions. Every effort will be made to use the more neutral and general term 'administrative agencies'. When the expression 'enforcing bodies' is used it refers to administrative agencies having a task with respect to control, investigation and possibly sanctioning of environmental crimes. The expression 'enforcing bodies' as used in this report, does not include enforcing bodies belonging to the judiciary system such as, for instance, the public prosecutor.

2.1 The right to start a prosecution before the criminal court

The first three questions (2(a) to (c)) relate to a topic of general interest in environmental law, being whether the public prosecutor has a sole competence to bring cases before the criminal court or whether individuals might have a role in bringing environmental cases before a criminal court themselves. Question 2(d) raises the question as to how, in practice, victims might play a role in that respect; question 2(e) concerns the issue as to what role victims can have in the public prosecution if they have no right to bring a criminal prosecutor themselves. Finally, 2(f) asks the question whether the fact that certain bodies and individuals might bring criminal prosecutions affects the role of the public prosecutor.

The following table summarizes the answers in the various country reports to questions 2(a) to (e):

Comments on these results are provided below. In this respect, it should also be mentioned that question 2(f) asked whether the fact that certain bodies and individuals can bring criminal prosecutions for environmental offences affects the role of the public prosecutor. This was almost unanimously denied for all legal systems where these possibilities to bring criminal prosecutions exist. Apparently, the fact that bodies and individuals can bring criminal prosecutions is not considered as having a negative impact on the role of the prosecutor. In Germany, a victim has certain rights of participation in criminal proceedings and the right of complaint against a decision of the prosecutor not to prosecute. Italy only refers to a positive influence in the sense that victims and enforcing bodies can help the prosecutor. Portugal refers to the fact that there is generally good co-ordination between environmental bodies and the public prosecutor.

2.2 The role of individuals, enforcing bodies, the police and the public prosecutor with respect to the investigation of environmental crime

Question 2(g) was a broader question, with respect to the role of individuals, enforcing bodies, police and the public prosecutor in the investigation of environmental crime. Most country reports refer first to the important role of

Table 2: The right to start a criminal prosecution

Country	a: **Enforcing bodies which may bring criminal prosecution**	b: **Can individuals bring criminal prosecution?**	c: **Permission of public prosecutor required?**	d: **Procedural advantages of criminal prosecution by victims**	e: **How can individuals participate in public prosecution, if not by bringing criminal prosecution?**
Austria	Police administrative organs;	Yes	No	Start with a report to police	—
Belgium	Public Ministry	Yes	No		—
Denmark	Public prosecutor	No	—	—	Report to police + witness + claim damages during trial
Finland	Public prosecutor (exceptionally: enforcing bodies)	Yes	No (but individuals + enforcing bodies have to wait)	Cases are rare	—
France	Public prosecutor and a specific administration	Yes: individuals have to require the public prosecutor to bring criminal prosecutions	No	Victims become the environmental watchdogs	—
Germany	Public prosecutor	No	(–)	(–)	as victims

Continued

Table 2 *Continued*

Country	a: Enforcing bodies which may bring criminal prosecution	b: Can individuals bring criminal prosecution?	c: Permission of public prosecutor required?	d: Procedural advantages of criminal prosecution by victims	e: How can individuals participate in public prosecution, if not by bringing criminal prosecution?
Italy	Public prosecutor	No	Yes	Inform	—
The Netherlands	Public prosecutor	No	No	—	Complaint against non-prosecution + ask for compensation in criminal procedure
Portugal	Public prosecutor	Yes. Both individuals and NGOs	Yes	Victims are assistants of prosecutor	—
Spain	Public prosecutor	Yes	Attorney's permission	—	—
England and Wales	Environment Agency	Yes	Generally: no		
Scotland	Public prosecutor	Yes	Generally: no		

the police. It is mentioned, for example, that for Austria, Denmark, Finland and Germany the preliminary investigation is primarily performed by the police. It is also mentioned that the criminal process usually starts with investigations performed by the police. In the United Kingdom the enforcing body carries out the investigations.

In addition, the role of individuals is also mentioned, but individuals apparently are mentioned as information-providers to the police or to enforcing bodies. Therefore, individuals may report environmental crime to the police or to enforcing bodies.

Almost all legal systems also stress the important role of enforcing bodies. They possess a great deal of expertise and technical information and provide information about administrative regulation. Therefore, their co-operation with the police is of crucial importance. For instance, Denmark, Finland, Germany and the Netherlands mention that the administrative authorities co-operate with the police as far as gathering evidence is concerned and that they provide technical assistance. In Germany, some 'Länder' have issued regulations with respect to the co-operation between authorities, sometimes including a duty to co-operate. It is, however, mentioned with respect to Italy, for instance, that the situation as far as the enforcing bodies is concerned is complicated, since there are four different competent bodies.

Finally, most country reports stress the importance of the public prosecutor as the one who leads the investigation. It is made clear (for instance, in the report on Finland, Germany and Italy) that it is primarily the public prosecutor who controls the investigation process and who gives instructions to the police. Thus, the public prosecutor is seen as the one who conducts the investigation and instructs the police. The country reports do not expressly mention whether enforcing bodies are subject to this control by the public prosecutor as well. In most countries, this is probably not the case. Most country reports, however, mention that there is generally good co-operation between enforcing bodies and the police during this investigation.

Finally, it should be mentioned that in some countries, such as Austria and Germany, a distinction is drawn between the administrative penalty procedure on the one hand and the criminal justice system on the other hand. This apparently has consequences both for the procedure to be followed and for the sanctions which might be applied.

2.3 The contribution of individuals and enforcing bodies to the proper regulation and enforcement of environmental law

The final theme within the context of Part 2 related to how enforcing bodies and individuals can contribute to the proper regulation and enforcement of environmental law.

As far as law making (regulation) is concerned, most country reports mention that individuals can contribute to the quality of environmental law which may lead to amendments of legislation.

As far as the enforcement of environmental law is concerned, most countries report that the most important role of individuals is simply to give notice of crime to enforcing bodies or to the police (see for instance the reports of Finland, Germany and the Netherlands). Individuals are apparently seen as being the first to discover an offence and who are therefore in a position to instigate an investigation (see for instance the Belgian report). The Italian country report explicitly mentions that the public awareness of environmental issues is so weak that this would also lead to a weakness of the contribution of individuals to the enforcement of environmental law.

Most country reports apparently consider the contribution of administrative agencies as important for the enforcement of environmental law. Some (for instance Denmark) mention that the special enforcing bodies are essential for the enforcement of environmental law; others stress once more the technical expertise of the enforcing bodies. They can therefore also provide important information to the public prosecution system (police and public prosecutor). The enforcing body in England and Wales is the prosecutor who is competent to take criminal proceedings through the courts.

Finally, it is also mentioned that many enforcement bodies not only play a role as far as the investigation is concerned (usually in co-operation with the police by providing technical assistance), but that they also have competence in most legal systems to deal with environmental offences through administrative measures. (For instance, Finland and the Netherlands mention it. It is obviously the case in all legal systems, although the contents and intensity of these administrative measures may differ.) However, the Netherlands explicitly mentions that the disadvantage of this administrative procedure is that these administrative enforcing bodies have the tendency to enter into overly lengthy negotiations with the offenders.

3. CRIMINAL PENALTIES

The third question relates to criminal penalties and asks what kind of criminal sanctions can be found in legislation and what type of sanctions are applied in practice.

3.1 Criminal sanctions that may be applied to those found liable for environmental offences and actual practice

The first question relates to the types of criminal sanctions that may be applied to those who violate environmental legislation. Obviously, this question does not immediately relate to the practice of environmental criminal law, but is more concerned more with the type of sanctions that can be found in material environmental criminal law.[4] The second question (3(b)) then relates to legal practice by asking which sanction would be most commonly applied and by seeking examples of levels of fines/present sentences. The third question (3(c)) is in fact the mirror image of 3(b) in that it asks what type of questions would be rarely applied, if at all. The answers in the country reports to the questionnaire are summarized in the following table:

3.2 (Un)popularity of specific sanctions

The questionnaire next asked why specific criminal penalties are apparently more popular in legal practice than others and why specific sanctions are very rarely applied. This will obviously be further addressed in the analysis, but at this stage it is interesting to address the issue on the basis of the answers to the questionnaire in the country reports.

Obviously, one important element in the selection of the punishment is, as is stated in the Finnish report, the quality of the offences. This might largely explain why fines are apparently more popular than prison sanctions. Another reason for the modest application of prison sanctions might be the reason given by Austria, this being that the task of criminal law is prevention. This could better be achieved through probation than through aprison sanction. The Dutch report also indicates why corporate sanctions (for instance the shut-down of a company) are not often applied in practice. These sanctions are felt as very heavy for the defendant and execution requires the co-operation of administrative enforcement bodies. Moreover, an administrative sanction with the same effect may already have been applied.

The French reporter also indicates that trade unions are often opposed to specific corporate sanctions, in spite of their deterrent properties. Moreover, the French reporter indicates that judges are rarely specialists of environmental law and might even have some kind of a respect for white-collar offenders.

In addition, the Italian and Portuguese country reports refer to a number of reasons related to the quality of environmental law which may explain the reluctance to apply sanctions other than fines. One reason is the preponderance of light cases and first offenders. Another is that there is as yet no relevant legal history since environmental criminal law is still relatively new. Judges are apparently still unfamiliar with this body of law. In addition, the

---

4 To some extent, this question was answered in the previous report (See Faure, M. and Heine, G., *supra*, 2000); overviews of applicable criminal sanctions in legislation can also be found in legal doctrine, to which we therefore refer.

Table 3: Criminal penalties

Country	Criminal sanction provided for in legislation	Sanctions most commonly applied	Examples	Rarely applied sanctions
Austria	– Judicial: * imprisonment up to 3 years * fines up to 360 day fines (max. 1,82m ATS) – Administrative fines	Fines	– 60 180-day fines – imprisonment 3–6 months (always probation)	All sanctions but fines plus imprisonment
Belgium	* imprisonment and/or fine * additional measures	Fines	– fines between €495.79 and €24,789.40	seizure of waste execution of specific measures ban on exploiting the establishment
Denmark	Main rule: fine Sometimes prison (if specific conditions are met) Max: 2 years Plus confiscation of profits	Fine plus confiscation of profits	– Average fine in agriculture: €538.66 – Average fine in industry: €2,949.17 – Detention rare (in practice: max 40 days)	Detention Loss of the right to carry out activities (just introduced)
Finland	Imprisonment, day fines, petty fines	Day fines	– Average 20–30 day fines plus imprisonment for unpaid day fines	Imprisonment
France	Fine or imprisonment	Fines	– Water pollution: €3,000.00	For individuals: imprisonment For legal entities: closing the factory

Continued

Table 3 *Continued*

Country	Criminal sanction provided for in legislation	Sanctions most commonly applied	Examples	Rarely applied sanctions
Germany	Rule: up to 3/5/15 years or fines – In case of negligence: max. 3 years or fine	Fines	– €10,225.80 – Imprisonment often suspended	3 or more years imprisonment
Italy	– Penal – Env. crimes: prison plus fine – Administrative: fine proportional to gravity of offence – Complementary sanctions: suspension of activity, obligation to pay for environmental damage or repair harm done	Administrative sanctions	Prison from 2 months to 2 years and/or fine	Imprisonment plus fines of substantial amounts
The Netherlands	Fine Imprisonment Dismissal of certain rights Shut-down of the company Confiscation Publication of the judgement Absorption of illegal gain Victim compensation Conviction to carry out what has been left undone Conviction to repair the harm	Fines	– Operating a small installation without licence: €453.78 – Minor water pollution: €453.78 – Illegal application of fertilizer: €680.67 – In severe cases: high fines (maximum €453,780) plus imprisonment	All sanctions but fines plus imprisonment

Continued

Table 3 *Continued*

Country	Criminal sanction provided for in legislation	Sanctions most commonly applied	Examples	Rarely applied sanctions
Portugal	Custodial sentences, commutable in fines	Fines	—	Custodial sentences
Spain	Prison: max. 4 years Fines Special disqualification from profession or post Closing of the company	Fines	—	—
United Kingdom	Imprisonment Community Penalties Fine	Fines	Fine from €71.30 – €1,425,923.00 Prison sentences rare (most often in waste cases)	Prison and community penalties

*The Italian reporteur probably referred to the sanctions provided for in legislation, and not the sanctions actually imposed in practice. This should hence be taken into account when comparing it with the other countries.

weak public awareness (in Italy) and the fact that it often concerns white-collar offenders who defend strong economic interests (Italy) might still have an impact on the attitude of courts towards environmental offences.

Finally, it should be stated that all reports, with the exception of Italy and the Netherlands, note that only courts have the jurisdiction to impose criminal sanctions. The Italian and Dutch reports also mention that the public prosecutor can take specific measures, an injunction for instance, but it is equally stated that this should not be considered a criminal sanction.

4. ADMINISTRATIVE SANCTIONS

4.1 General issues

This fourth question relates to repressive systems outside the core criminal law. Many countries have a long tradition with these kind of repressive side systems; others have adopted these systems within the last 15 years (Italy, Portugal). The questions deal with different kinds of sanctions levied not by the court, either by way of fixed penalties or as administrative fines. Table 4 summarizes the question as follows: the first category (non-criminal fines by administrative bodies) indicates whether the legal system concerned provides repressive sanctions outside true criminal law. Category 2 indicates the specific character of these sanctions, and category 3 the relationship to the criminal sanction. In category 4 (implementation) the question is whether such sanctions are frequently imposed. Category 5 provides the respondents with an opportunity to comment.

4.2 Sanctions, character and relationship to criminal sanctions

Most of the Member States provide for different kinds of administrative sanctions in their legal systems. However, repressive fines levied by an administrative agency is alien to Denmark and the Netherlands. Both countries have traditionally established only coercive fines, which means, for the Netherlands for example, that on the basis of Article 18.9 Environmental Management Act, the competent administrative body can issue a coercive fine (dwangsom). In case of non-compliance, the actor must pay a sum of money for the duration of the violation or for each violation of the Environmental Management Act. Furthermore, there is the possibility that the administrative body takes the ordered requirements on behalf of the owner and recovers the costs from the owner of the establishment. These legal figures are familiar to

Table 4: Administrative sanctions

Country	Non-criminal fines by administrative bodies	Character	Relationship to criminal sanctions	Implementation	Comment
Austria	administrative criminal fines by administrative bodies up to €218.02	'hermaphrodite' sanction	● administrative penal sanctions are imposed for minor violations ● lower requirements ● no double prosecution	higher importance than criminal law	● implementation not really satisfactory, accused previously convicted ● effect general rather than individual
Belgium	administrative fines by administrative bodies for a limited number of violations	purely administrative	enforcement of environmental regulation	rarely imposed	in respect of limited number of possibilities only small contribution
Denmark	no system of administrative penal law*	—	—	—	● environmental fee in political discussion* ● criminal law, accessory to administrative law, supports administrative enforcement*
Finland	non-criminal fine (vite), imposed by specific institutions (water court, local government, local environmental council)*	'hermaphrodite' sanction	● objectives: strengthening compliance with administrative orders, such as stopping the pollution ● fixed amount (no day-fines as in criminal law) €1,681.88	frequent	very effective, high amount, quick reaction

Continued

Table 4 *Continued*

Country	Non-criminal fines by administrative bodies	Character	Relationship to criminal sanctions	Implementation	Comment
France	– the préfet can impose administrative fines for classified installations – other systems of administrative fines exist	purely administrative sanction	administrative sanctions more efficient	not uncommon	very efficient: criminal system supports the administrative sanction
Germany	non-criminal fines by administrative bodies (exceptionally by criminal courts)	sanction non criminal; prerequisites follow some basic principles of criminal law (OwiG)	enforcement of administrative regulations, no imprisonment; only coercive detention to enforce fine.	very common	Contribution to the enforcement of environmental law
Italy	non-criminal fines by administrative bodies	administrative sanction (comparable to German OwiG)	minor contraventions, enforcement of administrative regulation relationship of minor to major	not frequently imposed	problem of implementation, lack of control
The Netherlands	only coercive fine	● administrative sanction ● sum for the departure from the violation of Environmental Management Act*	only influencing future behaviour in case of non-compliance*	criminal sanctions are comparable to administrative sanctions	on-going discussion to extend the possibilities imposing administrative penal sanctions by administrative agencies

Continued

Table 4 *Continued*

Country	Non-criminal fines by administrative bodies	Character	Relationship to criminal sanctions	Implementation	Comment
Portugal	non-criminal fines by administrative bodies	administrative measures	behaviour socially neutral, totally independent procedure	very frequent	more effective than criminal sanctions
Spain	non-criminal fees by administrative bodies	purely administrative	● no double prosecution ● administrative sanctions are assessed in economic issues	not reported	effective
Sweden	● non-criminal fine by administrative bodies* ● environmental fee*	● administrative sanction* ● administrative side sanction*	● enforcing compliance with administrative orders* ● independent of guilt*	– – rare*	– –
United Kingdom	no pure administrative fines, possibility of fixed penalties (not implemented). No power to administrative agencies	no distinction between criminal and administrative sanctions	variety of measures to ensure stricter regulatory control over operator, failure to comply with a prohibition notice is a criminal offence itself		—

*Added/corrected by the authors.

most other countries. Both in Denmark and in the Netherlands there is an ongoing political debate over extending the possibilities of the administrative agencies imposing environmental fines (Denmark) or administrative penal sanctions (The Netherlands). Currently in the Netherlands an experiment has been taking place with respect to a type of administrative fine that could in particular cases be imposed by administrative authorities for lesser infringements.[5]

Again, different wordings may lead to confusion. Usually the general word 'sanction' is used to refer to any kind of reaction whether administrative or criminal. When imposed by an administrative body or court these sanctions are simply referred to as 'administrative sanctions'. As far as monetary sanctions are concerned, again, the general word 'fine' is used, distinguishing between 'administrative' fines and 'criminal' fines. The word 'fee' or 'charge' is used for levies of a more fiscal nature.

All other Member States provide different kinds of administrative sanctions imposed by administrative bodies. For example, in Finland a fine (vite) can be imposed by specific institutions (such as water court, local government, local environmental council). In most other countries, it is an administrative body that is competent to impose the sanctions. In Belgium, administrative fines can be imposed only for a small number of environmental offences (such as not fulfilling the obligation to pay levies on manure production). The possibility of the Public Ministry requesting the offender pay a specified sum of money (settlement) plays an important role. This payment annuls the criminal proceedings. Specific systems (so-called Ordnungswidrigkeiten) have been established in Germany (since 1952, 1968) in Italy and in Portugal. France also has a system of fines that can be imposed as purely administrative sanctions, without the interference of a judge or a criminal court.

In the United Kingdom, a strict separation between criminal, penal and civil law is alien to the legal system. The Environment Agency in England and Wales has the responsibility for taking enforcement action, including serving enforcement notices or prohibition notices (as well as investigating and prosecuting environmental crime), the failure to fully comply with an enforcement/prohibition notice is a criminal offence in itself. In many areas of environmental law, the Environment Agency can carry out remedial work and reclaim the costs from the owner.

As a rule (apart from the UK), these administrative sanctions are fines. In

5 An evaluation of this experiment is discussed by Blomberg, A.B., Verberk, S. and Michiels, F.C.M.A., *Een gunstig aanbod. Een onderzoek naar de werking van het transactiebesluit milieudelicten*, Utrecht, Centrum voor Omgevingsrecht en Beleid, 2002.

some countries, there are fixed penalties (catalogues), while in others, legal frameworks are available. The amount of these administrative criminal fines differs extensively: in Austria, administrative bodies are empowered to impose fines up to ATS 3,000 (218.02 EUR), in Finland FMK 10,000 (1,618.88 EUR) and in Germany pursuant to the principal environmental statutes up to 100,000 DM (51,129.20 EUR) for natural persons and up to DM 1 million (511,292 EUR) in the case of a corporate fine (with possibilities of confiscation of proceeds to increase the amount).

In respect of the conditions under which these administrative criminal fines can be imposed, it is interesting to note that the prerequisites are sometimes similar to criminal law (Germany, Italy, Portugal), sometimes more so to administrative law. However, as a rule the strict criminal prerequisites, such as actor, causality, principle of ethical guilt, are at least partially relaxed. This allows it, for example in countries that up to now follow strictly the principle of ethical guilt in the criminal law, to establish corporate fines in these side systems (Germany, Italy, Portugal). In this process of relaxing the principles of criminal law, Sweden has been swiftest. The levying of a so-called environmental fee under the Environmental Protection Act is completely independent of guilt. The violation of an environmental regulation is only an incident for imposing a fee. However, most other countries require a violation and a specific kind of culpability. Furthermore, the European Court of Human Rights (1985) indicated minimum standards of due process: a double prosecution is against the law (explicitly in Austria and Spain).

Corresponding to the distinction between criminal law and administrative law, the character of these administrative criminal fines is the subject of never-ending discussion. As a rule, they are categorized as 'hermaphrodite' sanctions. However, Belgium, Italy, Portugal, Spain and Sweden define these fines as administrative measures. In Portugal in particular, this categorization is mainly influenced by De Figueiredo Dias, a famous scholar in Coimbra. According to Dias, whose opinion is generally adopted by the Portuguese legislator, the corresponding behaviour is socially neutral. Therefore, there is no place for criminal blameworthiness. Other legal systems try to explain that the relationship to criminal law is one of the minor to the major (Italy, Austria). However, in other countries it is obvious that it is not only minor offences that are incorporated in these side systems (for example Germany). Therefore, in some countries it is said that not the violation but the sanction is neutral – by legal fiction of the legislator (Germany). In any case, the main objectives of these fines are the enforcement of administrative regulation or orders by administrative bodies to ensure stricter regulatory control over the operator of a plant.

4.3 Implementation and comments

Most countries emphasize the importance of administrative criminal fines (as mentioned above, in the United Kingdom only sanctions in the unique form of criminal offences are available).[6] However, Italy and Sweden reply that such fines are seldom imposed. And in the Netherlands it is emphasized that criminal sanctions are comparable to administrative sanctions. The comments differ significantly. They are rather indicators for the view of the person/institution which has answered than a description of the situation in fact. In Austria and Italy, the implementation seems to be somewhat unsatisfactory; the Austrian respondent mentions that the accused was often previously convicted and that a preventive effect would be rather general than individual. In Italy, a lack of control is criticized, in so far as it seems to be a general problem of implementation of repressive measures. Other countries emphasize the effectiveness of administrative sanctions (Finland, Germany, Portugal and Spain). The Finnish comment mentions as an advantage the high amounts of the fines and the quick reaction. Also the French commentator argues that the prosecutor rarely prosecutes environmental crimes, so administrative sanctions can be considered far more efficient. These act, in the words of the French reporter, as deterrents to minor offenders.

5. EXISTENCE OF INSTRUMENTS WHICH PROHIBIT INDIVIDUALS FROM CARRYING OUT A SIMILAR ACTIVITY

5.1 General issues

This question deals with measures that may be imposed on an individual prohibiting him or her from carrying on a particular activity or a profession in the future. This is considered a very important instrument because in some cases the actor's attitudes may indicate that the law must prohibit that individual from carrying on certain activities endangering the environment and persons in the future. Table 5 summarizes the answers in six categories: the first provides the principal possibility of prohibition orders in the Member States. The second category deals with the nature of these prohibition orders (criminal/administrative). The third category answers the question regarding

---

[6] Recently, however, British law and economics scholars have argued that administrative sanctions should be introduced in UK environmental law as well. See e.g. Ogus, A. and Abbot, C., 'Sanctions for pollution: do we have the right regime?', *Journal of Environmental Law*, 2002, vol. 14, 283–300.

Table 5: Prohibition orders

Country	Principal possibility	Criminal/administrative	Imposed by	Examples	Implementation	Effectiveness/ operating under cover of another company
Austria	Yes	a) criminal side sanction b) administrative measure	criminal court administrative bodies	(–) threat of closing down a factory	rare	no answer
Belgium	Yes	a) criminal measure, even by anticipation b) administrative measure	a) criminal court b) administrative bodies	a) preliminary measure stopping pollution b) in case of non-compliance with orders	injunctions frequently applied	prohibition orders aimed against certain acts
Denmark	Prohibition to continue a profession*	criminal side sanction (§§ 78,79 P.C.)*	criminal court*	—	no*	
Finland	yes	criminal side sanction	criminal court	not in environmental cases	—	if used, it would be rather effective
France	In criminal law yes In administrative law no	only criminal	criminal court	the system is used for obtaining a new permit	—	it is easy to make a new legal entity in spite of prohibition order

Continued

Table 5 *Continued*

Country	Principal possibility	Criminal/administrative	Imposed by	Examples	Implementation	Effectiveness/ operating under cover of another company
Germany	prohibition to practice a profession	a) criminal measure (Maßregel)* b) administrative measure*	a) criminal court* b) administrative body*	a) in case of serious pollution; danger of recidivism; in the field of transboundary waste transport, waste disposal, unlawful operation of an installation	a) seldom imposed b) seldom ordered	no assessment
Italy	prohibition to practice a profession or an activity	a) sanction accessory to criminal sentence, broad spectrum* b) administrative measure*	a) criminal court* b) administrative body*	a) illegal maritime fishery	often imposed	not very effective, difficulties in investigating the real person responsible for an economic activity
The Netherlands	dismissal of certain rights	criminal side sanction	criminal court	—	very rarely imposed	not useful, the role of the convicted person can simply be taken over by someone else (in a company)

Continued

Table 5 *Continued*

Country	Principal possibility	Criminal/administrative	Imposed by	Examples	Implementation	Effectiveness/ operating under cover of another company
Portugal	prohibition from practising a profession or activities	side sanctions to sanctions of the OwiG	● administrative bodies, appeal to Criminal Court ● by criminal court	—	very frequently	—
Spain	yes	administrative	competent administrative body	—	frequent application	preventive measure
Sweden	prohibition carrying on a business*	*sanction sui generis**	● requested by the prosecution ● separate court procedure*		rarely in environmental cases	—
United Kingdom	prohibition notice, in cases of serious risk of personal injury or harm to the environment to stop the operation of the activity	first instance administrative measure, or if violated may become a criminal sanction	● administrative bodies, contravention of prohibition notice is a crime ● criminal court	integrated pollution control, waste control, radioactive substances; water pollution	frequently imposed on legal persons (!), conditioning its activities	applies to the legal person

*Added/corrected by the authors.

which institution serves the notice. The next categories provide examples and implementation. The last category deals with the specific problem of the practical effectiveness, given the possibility of an individual operating under cover of another company or legal entity.

5.2 Legal possibilities, character and institutions

As a rule, the principle of serving an order prohibiting an individual from performing a particular activity or profession in the future is adopted in the Member States. In many European countries, two different kinds of prohibition orders exist: one in the sphere of the criminal law and a second in the sphere of administrative law (Austria, Belgium, Germany, Italy). In Denmark the prohibition of continuing the polluting activity is an administrative measure. However, prohibiting activities which might be particularly polluting can be imposed by a criminal court. In the Netherlands prohibition orders are within the domain of criminal law, in Portugal it is exclusive to administrative penal law (Ordnungs-widrigkeitenrecht). In Sweden it is a sanction *sui generis*. The countries with double competences have established different prerequisites for imposing these prohibition orders: as a rule, to impose prohibition orders in the context of criminal law, the conditions are much stricter than on the basis of administrative law. The competent authority corresponds to the nature of this measure. The criminal court is competent to impose the prohibition as a criminal side sanction. Administrative bodies are empowered to impose administrative measures. In any case, the actor or the owner has an opportunity to appeal to the criminal court or to an administrative court. Sweden has a unique system. The prosecutor requests a prohibition from exercising a business, available as a separate court procedure. The United Kingdom, which allows prohibition orders for stopping the operation of a particular plant as an administrative measure or as an additional criminal sanction, has given a special status to this order: contravening a prohibition notice is a crime. All notices are intended to stop the operation of the activity not to stop an individual from operating in a particular profession. In some countries courts can impose a ruling by anticipation (Belgium).

5.3 Implementation, examples and special questions

In most countries, prohibition orders do not play a prominent role (Austria, Denmark, Germany, the Netherlands, Sweden). Sometimes, it is said that there are difficulties in investigating the person who is in fact responsible for an economic activity. Others emphasize that the role of the convicted person can simply be assumed by someone else in a company. Therefore, there is no answer which provides legal remedies against continuing operation under cover of another company.

Nevertheless, prohibition orders seem to play an important role in Italy, Portugal and the United Kingdom. The relevant cases are mostly waste disposal (United Kingdom), illegal maritime fishing (Italy) and serious pollution and illegal waste disposal especially if there is a danger of recidivism (Germany). Of special interest is the situation in the United Kingdom. It is not necessary to find the person who is in fact responsible for an economic activity because a prohibition notice is served upon a company. The notice stops that particular activity from being carried out and specifies the steps to be taken by the operator to remedy the contravention and the time period within which to do so. Breach of a prohibition order is a criminal offence.

6. TRANSFRONTIER POLLUTION INCIDENTS

The sixth question relates to transfrontier pollution, incidents which would have occurred in the particular Member State. The question was asked as to whether there have been any specific cases of transfrontier pollution which led to criminal investigation and prosecution. Particular attention was of course given to the question of whether these transboundary pollution cases had given rise to particular problems for the investigating and prosecuting bodies. With a view to possible changes in the future, the country report also examined whether the existing formal treaties were considered sufficient to enable an effective investigation and/or extradition.

The answers to the various questions as given in the country report are summarized in the following table:

7. CRIMINAL LIABILITY FOR ENVIRONMENTAL OFFENCES BY PUBLIC SERVANTS AND PUBLIC AUTHORITIES

7.1 General issues

It is well-known that public servants and public authorities have become a great power in protecting the environment by granting permits to polluters, imposing conditions on activities that pollute the environment and controlling corresponding activities. Therefore, it is often said that not the parliament, but the administrative authorities are the real key-institutions in the

Table 6: Transfrontier pollution incidents

Country	Description of transfrontier pollution incidents	Particular problems	Are formal treaties sufficient?
Austria	Great water pollution case with Slovenia. Both countries started investigation + prosecution	Difficult to obtain essential information from neighbouring countries	Very difficult obtaining essential info
Belgium	* illegal transport of waste * illegal trading in illegal species	* time-consuming procedures * dependant on foreign authority * sovereignty	Rogatory commissions are often not possible
Denmark	illegal transfrontier shipment of waste and oil spills	—	—
Finland	One case: river pollution from Finland to Russia; two directors sentenced in Finland. No problem through transfrontier character; Russian authorities not involved	Problems with 100 cases in 1997 of marine oil pollution. Aeroplane surveillance; reporting to flag-state as well	Marpol does not allow stopping a ship on open sea, so investigation delayed
France	Problems with Switzerland, Belgium, Luxemburg, Germany and Spain, but mostly not criminal	Co-operation between neighbouring States is good	No, because the treaties do not include criminal law
Germany	Several cases; especially waste disposal, water pollution import of nuclear materials, endangered species	Investigation is difficult in waste and water pollution cases	– Amendments of European instruments in international co-operation are to be expected – Co-operation must be deepened at level of intensity, not at organizational level

Continued

Table 6 *Continued*

Country	Description of transfrontier pollution incidents	Particular problems	Are formal treaties sufficient?
Italy	Sinking of 80 ships with radioactive waste	– No assistance – No enforcement by Interpol – Lack of jurisdiction of EU – Absence of collaboration in exchange for info	No. For instance, Greek captain went to Greece. No support from Greece and no investigation
The Netherlands	Two main cases: - import of household waste with export to third-world countries. – violation of Reg. 259/93	– Getting info from authorities of other States difficult: takes time + do not receive requested info – Different policy in other countries affects attitude of authorities – Generally co-operation between neighbouring States is good	Yes, sufficient
Portugal	No particular problems	– River pollution between Portugal and Spain	Yes
Spain	No case	—	—
United Kingdom	No case	—	—

field of protection of the environment. Furthermore, at least in Member States such as Germany, it has to be regarded that the parliament has lost some power to enact strict prohibitions in the field of environmental and technical law and (conversely) the local authorities are in a catch-all position ('umgekehrte Wesentlichkeitstheorie'). Therefore, in the last twenty years criminal law has turned towards public servants and public authorities to ensure adequate environmental protection.

Table 7 contains the answers of the different Member States. Category 1 deals with the principal possibility of criminal liability, category 2 with the prerequisites. To take into consideration other effective measures, category 3 allows for explanations. Category 4 records the implementation and category 5 describes the answers with respect to problems of criminal liability of public servants. Table 7 is not intended to deal with problems where communities are running private plants.

7.2 Criminal liability, prerequisites and other liabilities

Apart from Sweden, where no information was available, all Member States concerned provide criminal provisions in respect of criminal liability of public servants. However, two categories must be distinguished. The first is the rather traditional abuse of administrative power, the other the criminal liability for environmental offences.

The majority of Member States are merely familiar with the traditional model (Austria, Denmark, Finland, United Kingdom). In Austria, abuse of administrative power is a crime. Danish law provides that cases of gross violations of administrative duties in carrying out a public task are considered crimes. If a Danish municipality commits environmental crime, in principle the same rules apply as in respect of corporate or personal liability. Moreover, the State can be held criminally liable. For instance, the Ministry of Defence has been fined for oil spills at a yard for tanks. Finland has established a general obligation to perform services, and a contravention is considered a crime. The abuse of specific status is as much a prerequisite as intent, any disadvantage is sufficient. This seems to be on the same lines as that found in the common law (United Kingdom).

In Italy, the illegal omission of an official act is criminalized; following the opinion of scholars, participating in an environmental offence is a crime. This leads directly to the situation in the other countries. In Germany and in the Netherlands the courts have taken the initiative, following the leading opinion of scholars. In Germany in 1993, the federal Supreme Court developed criminal responsibility of public servants. However, criminal liability for environmental offences is in practice limited to water and soil pollution and waste

Table 7: Criminal liability servants and public authorities

Country	Criminal liability	Prerequisites	Other liabilities	Implementation	Problems of criminal liability
Austria	abuse of administrative power	—	compensation	no practical meaning	—
Belgium	liability for environmental offences	power of decision, power to stop the infringement	—	?	(–)
Denmark	gross violation of administrative duties in carrying out of a public task*	—	—	no practical meaning*	—
Finland	general obligation to perform services, contravention is a crime	abuse of the specific status; intent, any disadvantage	—	rarely, in cases of improper supervision of companies	improving responsibility
France	in theory: yes in practice: no	only in case of corruption, complicity or incitement of a civil servant can criminal liability be invoked	—	—	since July 2000 civil servants can only be held liable in case of a fault characterized as personal

Continued

Table 7 *Continued*

Country	Criminal liability	Prerequisites	Other liabilities	Implementation	Problems of criminal liability
Germany	developed by the Federal Supreme Court, responsibility of individuals	partially limited to water pollution and waste disposal Illegal permission, illegal non-retracting of permission, illegal non-intervention against pollution; however: wide administrative discretion. Intent or negligence*	disciplinary liability liability for the damage	sentencing in clear cases, many preliminary investigations*	strong tendency to cover themselves by calling in superior authorities
Italy	illegal omission of an official act (Art. 328 c.p.); participation in an environmental offence*			very rare*	no deterrence because of flexible legal prerequisites*
Netherlands	developed by the Federal Supreme Court			in clear cases	important in respect of a democratic control of the public authority
Portugal	developed in doctrine	illegal damaging of the nature, illegal pollution of environmental media		no cases	—

Continued

Table 7 *Continued*

Country	Criminal liability	Prerequisites	Other liabilities	Implementation	Problems of criminal liability
Spain	in general: illegal decision of a public servant, especially for environmental crimes illegal decisions, illegal vote for a decision, illegal report*	intent, actions against environment*	—	set in force 1996*	—
Sweden	?	?	?	?	?
United Kingdom	government departments immune, individuals not, nor are government agencies for instance Environment Agency		reviewing the administrative decisions, High Court can force the administrative bodies to remake their decisions	very rare	—

*Added/corrected by the authors.

disposal. Three cases can be differentiated: illegally granting a permit, illegally not retracting a permit and, finally, illegally not intervening to prevent pollution. However, administrative law grants, as a rule, wide discretion to public services. Therefore, criminal liability occurs only in cases of clearly illegal behaviour. This criminal responsibility is not limited to intentional behaviour; even in case of negligence resulting in illegal pollution, criminal sanctions can be imposed. In Belgium, responsibility can be imposed on civil servants who had the decision-taking power and the authority to stop the infringement. In the Netherlands in 1998, the Hoge Raad developed a similar criminal responsibility of civil servants in case of carrying out a specific governmental task. The State itself is, however, still immune from criminal liability; this immunity extends to civil servants working for the State. The Spanish legislator was the swiftest to react in 1996. In Spain, traditionally taking an illegal decision by a public servant is a crime. However, the new Spanish criminal code intended to eliminate loopholes in the criminal responsibility of public servants. Therefore, especially for environmental crimes, several provisions deal with criminal sanctions imposed on civil servants in cases of indirectly causing pollution, not only in cases of taking an illegal decision, but also for giving a false report to a person with the authority to take decisions (indirect authority). Even illegally voting for an administrative decision (in the context of a collective decision of a group of persons) is a crime if, based on this illegal decision, a person causes pollution. However, in contrast to Germany, only intentional behaviour is sanctioned.

There is mostly no answer to the question whether public agencies as such can be held criminally liable. However, in the United Kingdom the answer is clear. Government departments are immune, individuals not. Hence, local authorities and the environment agency can be held criminally liable. In the Netherlands, the State is immune. In Germany, non-penal fines can also be imposed on public corporations and other public entities. In France, there is formally no immunity for civil servants or public authorities. However, civil servants working for public legal entities can only be held liable in cases of faults that can be characterized as personal or in case of an evident personal lapse in duty. This was the result of an amendment in 2000. Before this amendment, the French reporter indicates that local councillors and mayors even refused to stand again as candidates in elections because of the risk of personal criminal liability.

In respect of other liabilities, it must be mentioned that disciplinary liability seems to be available in all Member States. For some countries, it is noted that illegal decisions of an administrative body can lead to compensation. The British report adds that the central governmental departments (crown bodies) can face a declaration in the High Court that their act is unlawful. Central government, local authorities and the environment agency can also face civil claims in the High Court if they have acted in breach of statutory duty (tort) or misfeasances while carrying out of public duties take place. In addition, the United Kingdom has a very highly developed system of traditional review – as do most other European countries – whereby individuals and companies can review decisions of the central government, local authorities or the environment agencies on procedural grounds. The High Court can force the administrative bodies to review or retake their decisions.

7.3 Implementation and problems of criminal liability

The answers referring to the enforcement of criminal provisions on liability of civil servants have one common denominator: taking the number of convictions as a measure, criminal liability of civil servants does not play an important role in European legal systems. In particular, no cases are reported in Austria, Belgium, Denmark, Portugal and Spain. In the other countries, sentencing cases are reportedly very rare (Germany, Italy, Netherlands, Spain, England and Wales). However, there is a tendency to impose criminal sanctions in severe cases. For example, in Germany two leading decisions of the federal Supreme Court deal first with a decision against the administrative law by a civil servant indirectly causing water pollution and secondly a false report given by a civil servant of a technical administrative agency, resulting in a wrongful decision of an administrative agency competent for waste disposal. Furthermore, many preliminary investigations have been taken against civil servants suspected of indirectly causing environmental pollution by illegal administrative permits or by illegal non-intervention to prevent pollution.

The question of whether the criminal liability of civil servants may affect the way they conduct their affairs is answered in different ways. Austria, Denmark, Portugal, Spain, Sweden and the United Kingdom did not answer. The Finnish reporter emphasizes that criminal liability of civil servants may improve their responsibility. In Germany, a tendency to protect themselves by calling in superior authorities is observed. The Netherlands' questionnaire underlines the importance in respect of a democratic control of the public authority. However, in Italy a deep scepticism against criminalizing the actions of civil servants is observed. It is said that in respect of flexible legal prerequisites, no deterrent effect will take place.

8. MISCELLANEOUS

The questions which were raised in the miscellaneous section relate to two separate issues. Questions (a) and (b) relate to the effectiveness of administrative sanctions and to whether minor breaches, for instance technical breaches of a permit without environmental harm are, in general, tolerated. These questions are still somewhat related. Question (c) relates to a different topic, this concerning the role played by intelligence services in environmental investigation. The latter question relates to the issue how information can be gathered on environmental crimes during a preliminary investigation.

The answers to questions (a) and (b) are summarized as follows:

The answers in the country reports regarding the role of the intelligence services, are summarized in the following table:

Table 8: Margin of discretion in prosecution of environmental offences

Country	Effectiveness of administrative sanctions	Is there tolerance for minor breaches?
Austria	—	No tolerance + tolerance does not affect effectiveness of criminal prosecution
Belgium	Administrative sanctions are as effective as criminal	* no systematic tolerance * laxer attitude at municipal level
Denmark	Will depend on the contents of the administrative sanctions	Also formal breaches without harm should be fined = intent of legislator, but tolerance might influence level of fine
Finland	Difficult to compare; publicity (bad PR) has strong deterrent impact	Yes, there is tolerance for technical breaches of permit
France	Administrative sanctions are really efficient	Yes, but not for individual offenders in the fields of fishing, hunting or cruelty to animals

Continued

Table 8 *Continued*

Country	Effectiveness of administrative sanctions	Is there tolerance for minor breaches?
Germany	Yes, because: – they can be used against companies – max 1m. DM	Administrative bodies often first use effective administrative tools (for instance strengthening law using 'soft' measures). For minor breaches, environmental bodies may negotiate with operator
Italy	Administrative in principle more effective, because: – direct application – damages wealth of offender but: lack of control	Yes, tolerance also because of collusion with public authorities
The Netherlands	In general, administrative sanctions are effective, but: administrative bodies not eager to impose sanctions	– Yes, public prosecutor tolerates minor breaches as a matter of policy – Government wants to limit tolerance by administrative bodies (for greater breaches) – But administrative bodies seek agreement, believing individuals + firms are trustworthy
Portugal	Yes + administrative sanctions more effective	No tolerance
Spain	Not too much	Sanction is imposed in line with degree of breach + with damage caused
United Kingdom	No	Minor incidents: only warning as (hopefully) no environmental effect

Table 9: Role of intelligence services

Country	Role of intelligence services in environmental investigation	Co-operation between intelligence services, police + enforcement bodies	Can info supplied by intelligence services be used in criminal procedure?
Austria	Competent authority = minister of the interior	—	All supplied info can be used
Belgium	rare	—	—
Denmark	No	Links could be established in a specific cases, if necessary	—
Finland	No	—	—
France	No, except in the marginal field of ecological terrorism	—	—
Germany	No	Police relies on info from enforcement bodies	—
Italy	Yes, especially for environmental security	Police receives input to open preliminary investigation from intelligence services	—
The Netherlands	Important role	They work together with police, but different role: less secret info	Info can generally be used
Portugal	—	Yes, satisfactory co-ordination + co-operation	—
Spain	—	Yes, good collaboration	Info supplied can be used
United Kingdom	Yes, in major waste transfer cases	Problem of protection of anonymity	No need to disclose sensitive info in proceedings

EVALUATION OF THE ANSWERS

1. CRIMINAL LIABILITY OF CORPORATIONS FOR ENVIRONMENTAL OFFENCES

1.1 Corporate criminal liability

In general, it can be said that the increase in global environmental pollution and malfunctions in industrial enterprises give rise to difficult liability issues in any legal system. The issue concerns new types of risks resulting from complex technical, economic and social considerations. The points of departure in this discussion of corporate criminal liability are at variance: on the one hand, the Anglo-Saxon legal sphere and others influenced thereby have had the most experience with notions of collective responsibility, on the other hand, until a few years ago, the axiom '*societas delinquere non potest*' dominated the history of continental European criminal law. Despite these contrasts, common ground does exist in Europe. Whereas currently corporate criminal liability is very common in the United Kingdom, the Netherlands, France and Denmark, Finland followed the new Scandinavian line in 1995. Moreover, Belgium introduced criminal liability of legal entities in 1999. Furthermore, there is a political debate emerging over establishing corporate criminal liability in Germany and Spain. For example, in Germany the Ministry of Justice of Hessia presented a draft for discussion, establishing criminal liability for enterprises in the winter of 1997–1998 and a commission on the reform of sanctions established by the Federal Minister of Justice included this topic in its agenda. And on the scientific level, there is a intense debate in Germany, Italy, Portugal, Spain and Austria.

This development in Europe is indeed a reaction to international incentives: the Convention for the protection of the environment by criminal law, drafted by the Council of Europe,[1] emphasizes the need for sanctions imposed on legal persons. On the same lines lies the OECD Convention of 17 December 1997 on combating bribery of foreign public officials in international business transactions.[2] The protocol for the protection of the financial interests of the EC stresses that the parties establishing criminal liability of enterprises apply at least monetary sanctions. It leaves discretion to the countries to take other non-criminal measures. Irrespective of these latest trends, many countries which are dominated by the classical doctrine of ethical guilt have established other non-criminal and distinct forms of influencing enterprises. Ten years ago in Austria, the legislator established the possibility of confiscating illegal benefits gained by legal persons, a possibility which also exists in other countries like Germany, which until now has seen no legal possibility in respect of the doctrine of ethical guilt, of criminalizing enterprises.

However, apart from the legal possibilities of confiscation, many countries have developed side systems, so-called administrative penal law or Ordnungswidrigkeiten, for sanctioning enterprises. This is the case with the so-called 'Verbandsgeldbuße' in Germany and Portugal, a kind of contravention of administrative regulation, similar to the regulatory offences in the Anglo-Saxon countries. Furthermore, even Italy, a country whose Constitution seems to hinder criminal liability (Art. 27 Italian Constitution), has established administrative penal measures against enterprises, these include fiscal fines, suspension of activities, and compensation or restoration. The Austrian legislator still retains the classical instrument of the Roman law family. The legal person is co-debtor of a fine (in administrative penal law). The reason for this development of corporate sanctions in side systems is that these administrative penal systems are to be regarded as not having a true criminal nature. Mostly, these systems are 'hermaphrodite' in nature, combining characteristics from criminal and administrative law.

A key condition for imposing these different kinds of sanctions on enterprises is either the recognition of the wrongdoing of high managerial agents

---

1 This convention has been adopted on 4 November 1998 and can be found in annex 3.

2 See on these international developments also Pieth, M., 'Criminal responsibility of legal and collective entities: international developments', in Eser, A., Heine, G. and Huber, B. (eds.), *Criminal responsibility of legal and collective entities, Max Planck Institute for foreign and international criminal law*, Freiburg im Breisgau, 1999, 113–117 as well as Mörenschlager, M., 'Developments on the international level', in Eser, A., Heine, G. and Huber, B. (eds.), *Criminal responsibility of legal and collective entities, Max Planck Institute for foreign and international criminal law*, Freiburg im Breisgau, 1999, 89–103.

(ordering a violation) or the violation of supervisory duties, even by delegates. However, many countries are broadening the categories of persons who can be held liable. Therefore, taken as a European standard, the crime of an employee is sufficient in the case of a violation of supervisory duties by higher representatives. Furthermore, many countries are willing to accept corporate criminal liability in cases where the person responsible for an individual fault cannot be identified. In some countries, a certain group of persons in charge will be held responsible. In England and Wales, no fault needs to be proved because environmental offences are offences of strict liability. However, the lack of a clear doctrine and key principles in these cases is an ongoing problem in all Member States. A solution might be found in following the line that the European Court of Justice in anti-trust legislation has taken. For example, one specific problem is attributing *mens rea* in cases where no individual is criminally liable. The European Court of Justice – as a rule – refers to the capacity and possibility of the enterprise as a whole. This could mean that, in respect of assuming intent or negligence, it is not the restricted knowledge of an individual but the broader capacity of an enterprise as a group of persons with the appropriate legal and necessary technical capacities that is important.

What is remarkable is Sweden's environmental fee, which is independent of the guilty behaviour of an enterprise or an individual. Violation of the law and benefit to the company is sufficient. However, in respect of influencing behaviour of companies, it is an ongoing problem to establish principles of absolute liability.

Another crucial point is that in many countries there are only rare cases of corporate criminal liability, Especially in Germany where the non-criminal corporate fine of the Ordnungswidrigkeitengesetz has not played a significant role in the field of protection of the environment. Many reasons may be mentioned. In the field of the administrative penal code, administrative agencies have on the whole wide discretion to impose sanctions. The emphasis in criminal investigations on the criminal responsibility of individual natural persons may in practice lead to neglect of the issue of corporate liability. The practical consequences are that only in cases of persistent acts involving gross violations there seems to be a need for stricter sanctions. Furthermore, the conflict between the economy and ecology is hard to resolve at a local administrative level. Finally, the principle of co-operation between administrative agencies and enterprises often hinders stricter enforcement. In so far as that is concerned, it raises a conflict of principles.

On the other hand, in the UK, corporate liability plays a significant role in compliance with the law by measures of fines and costs and restoration.

Nearly all cases prosecuted are against the company because of strict liability. Prosecution of directors is rare, and employees are almost never prosecuted.

1.2 Criminal liability of directors and managers

All countries indicated an acceptance of the criminal liability of directors and managers. However, the criminal liability of high managerial agents indirectly contributing to committing environmental offences is a newer development in most European countries. In some countries, such as Germany, the federal Supreme Court has taken the initiative; in other countries, such as Finland, the legislator has established a special provision. Therefore, the prerequisites and limits of criminal liability are still in discussion. In many countries, the prerequisites under the criminal code are more restricted than in administrative penal systems. This is for example the situation in Germany (e.g. in relation to the administrative offence of violating supervisory duties) and Austria. One reason is that in the side systems, mostly lesser sanctions are available, therefore the high criminal standards can be relaxed. Another reason is that in these side systems the objectives of the law are different and the elements of liability are influenced by issues of other disciplines of law, such as civil liability and administrative statutes.

In any event it appears that legislators and courts are developing and expanding the way in which they pursue the criminal liability of high managerial agents. This development must be seen in the context of corporate liability. One problem is that in decentralized, large-scale enterprises, the limits of traditional criminal law are obvious. Therefore, a new key question is the balancing of the responsibility of individuals with the liability of legal persons. The spheres of responsibility of individuals and organizations can coincide, but must of necessity diverge for the simple reason that the potential scope of an enterprise is completely different, especially in view of its powerful legal and technical departments, the temporal and spatial continuity of the organization as a whole and its incomparable social power. The EC-jurisdiction on anti-trust has developed leading principles and decisive categories of liability of enterprises, which means, for example, that in the description of subjective elements, the special potential of enterprises is taken into account. Furthermore, 'guilt' as the specific responsibility of the enterprise should be understood in the sense that the 'material disposition or attitude' of the firm prevented it from taking legal co-ordination and reorganization decisions and allowed a defective risk management with serious socially detrimental effects to prevail. Faulty decisions over time could therefore replace individual guilt. Following this route would allow two types of criminal responsibility to exist: a comprehensive liability, which is on the enterprise itself, and a closer responsibility in the case of faulty single decisions or orders by intent, or gross negligence, which is on individuals.

2. THE ROLE OF ENFORCING BODIES AND OF INDIVIDUALS IN CONNECTION WITH ENVIRONMENTAL OFFENCES

2.1 General issues

This second question relates to the crucial point in the enforcement of environmental criminal law, being the various tasks of individuals (both citizens and NGOs), the police, enforcing bodies and the office of the public prosecutor. Obviously, some of the elements in the answers to this question do not only relate to environmental crime. The question, for instance, of whether individual citizens or NGOs have the right to bring a criminal prosecution directly is heavily entrenched in the national criminal procedure of the various Member States. However, it is equally clear that an answer to this question does influence the enforcement of environmental criminal law as well. Nevertheless, a number of specific aspects concerning the relationship between the various parties mentioned will play significant roles, especially in environmental cases. In that respect, one can for instance refer to the highly technical nature of the environmental risk in general as well as of material environmental criminal law. Since in most countries crimes are still of the abstract endangerment type, whereby the mere violation of emission standards is criminalized for instance, the public prosecutor (and his or her police force) will to a large extent have to rely on the expertise of specific enforcement bodies, who are better equipped to examine for instance whether the specific emission standard was in fact violated or not. These kind of issues, related to the link between administrative regulations and to the technical nature of the abstract endangerment crimes inherent in environmental criminal law, are of course more typical for this field.

In this evaluation of the answers, some of the general issues and interests that play a role concerning this topic shall be briefly addressed and an attempt will be made to identify a few trends in the answers. Obviously, the information provided in the answers is a limiting factor and thus it is possible only to go beyond that to a limited extent to elaborate on the role of enforcing bodies and of individuals at a more general level.

The answers to the questions made clear that individuals, NGOs and enforcing bodies do indeed play a role at various levels of the investigation and prosecution of environmental crime. The strength of this role, however, varies largely between the Member States and usually depends on specific conditions laid down in procedural law or environmental legislation, which was obviously not addressed in detail in the answers to the questionnaire.

2.2 The role of individuals, enforcing bodies, the police and the public prosecutor with respect to the investigation of environmental crime

2.2.1 Powers of control versus investigation of a suspected crime

Turning first to the enforcement of environmental legislation through criminal law, it will be noted that according to the answers to question 2(g), in almost all Member States the traditional police forces still play an important role in the preliminary investigation. England and Wales are exceptions to this general finding as the police plays no role. The Environment Agency is both the investigating and the prosecuting body. It is made equally clear that the police often does not act on its own initiative, but rather based on the fact that a presumption of a violation of environmental legislation has been made clear to them, either by individuals (who suspect that an environmental crime has been committed) or by enforcing bodies. In that respect, in many Member States (although this issue is not explicitly addressed in the answers), the powers of the police are to some extent more limited as far as the beginning the preliminary investigation is concerned than those of the second party involved, the enforcing bodies. This does not exclude police observation from becoming the starting point for such investigation (in one empirical study in Germany, 21% compared with 45% of private and 27% of administrative authorities complained). The police usually is only legally allowed to become active after there has been a *suspicion* that an environmental crime has been committed. In that case, the procedural law of the Member States (or specific environmental legislation) usually grants the right to the police to investigate on the basis of the suspicion of the particular crime.

The powers of enforcing bodies, however, in some cases go further. They mostly have far-reaching powers of control, which means that they could for instance visit premises and inspect whether or not the specific environmental legislation was accurately followed by the enterprise (or individual) involved. These powers of control are obviously of high importance, given the traditionally hidden nature of environmental crime. This means that if there were no powers to inspect and the police or other authorities could only become active in a preliminary investigation after a crime had been detected (for instance through a report by an individual to the police), the detection rate would inevitably be too low. Precisely in order to take into account this hidden character of many environmental crimes, far-reaching powers have been granted enforcing administrative bodies to monitor whether the environmental legislation has been upheld correctly. An important feature of these powers of control is, therefore, that these can also be applied, even when there is no suspicion that an environmental crime has been committed. Obviously, in many cases the inspection carried out by the enforcing bodies may lead to the finding that the provisions of environmental legislation have been violated, in which case there is of course a suspicion of a crime, where the ordinary police may step in.

Not all Member States have a clear distinction between the inspection (executed before there is any suspicion) and an investigation (which takes place after a suspicion has arisen). Even in countries which stick to the principle of separation of preventive and repressive powers, such as in Germany, the frontiers are nebulous. Moreover, in some Member States the question of whether only administrative enforcing bodies can exercise these rights of control (and not the ordinary police) is debated. In some countries (for instance to a limited extent in Belgium), the ordinary police can also exercise some powers of control. Sometimes there are objections made to this, since powers of control obviously impose a serious infringement of the freedom of the citizens. This question of the extent of the powers of inspection and the question over to whom these should be granted shows that already at this initial stage a balancing interests will have to take place between the need to control environmental crime on the one hand and the respect for the rule of law on the other. From the need to enforce criminal law, powers of inspection are obviously necessary (given the risk of an otherwise too low detection rate), but the question arises as to how these can be kept within reasonable limits, taking into account the rule of law. One point seems to be clear; if unconditioned use of information achieved by means of inspection is available for purposes of criminal law, special safeguards of criminal law are pushed away. Different solutions may be available in respect of the kind of information and the kind of offender (natural person or collective entity).

2.2.2 Technical expertise and co-operation

Enforcing bodies of administrative agencies usually do not only intervene in the enforcement of criminal law through their powers of inspection. In the stage of the preliminary investigation, where the police gets involved to investigate the suspicion of an environmental crime, civil servants of the enforcing bodies will also play a considerable role. This, once more, has to do with the often technical nature of the provisions in environmental criminal law and the links with administrative law. The abstract endangerment provisions often require that it should be proven, for example, certain chemical substances were emitted in amounts that were too great. Often, only the enforcing bodies have access to the methods to bring this proof. Given the fact that the ordinary police does not have this specialized knowledge, very often the enforcing bodies will co-operate with the police during the preliminary investigation and provide technical assistance.

Most countries report that no specific problems arise as far as co-operation between the police and the specific enforcing bodies is concerned. Generally, this co-operation is characterized as good. Given the technical expertise of the enforcing bodies, some even report that the contribution of the enforcing bodies is indeed essential for the enforcement of environmental criminal law. Obviously some respondents (for instance Belgium) noticed that the degree of co-operation might differ from one administration to another. Some administrations only comply with requests for technical assistance from the police on the condition that the request stems formally from the examining judge or the public prosecutor.

Problems could, however, arise with respect to the specific legal position of these enforcing bodies. Formally, in most countries it is indeed the public prosecutor who still controls the preliminary investigation. This means that when the police are carrying out a preliminary investigation, they principally do so under the supervision of the public prosecutor who also guides the investigation. Less clear is whether for instance the public prosecutor would also have a right to give orders to the public enforcing bodies. Usually, this appears to be denied, given the separation of powers (this is different in Germany in relation to administrative offences the investigation of which is assumed by the prosecutor). Although the specific legal regimes in the Member States may differ in that respect, usually it appears the police must rely on the voluntary co-operation of the administrative enforcing bodies. However a duty of co-operation may exist in certain areas, too. Such a duty may be part of the rules of criminal procedure or of administrative law (e.g., in Germany in several state administration regulations). Specific problems in that respect are not reported. The reader should also bear in mind that within the Member States the roles of enforcing bodies on the one hand and police on the other may be different in practice. Some countries may rely more on police officers, also for the preliminary investigation, and try for instance to cope with the problem of lacking expertise by building specific environmental police corps; other countries seem to rely more heavily on the technical expertise of the specific enforcing bodies and seem to use the police more when it comes to the need to apply specific police powers, which the enforcing bodies could not. These specific differences were, however, not debated in the country reports.

2.2.3 *Administrative sanctions*

With respect to the role of administrative bodies, it should also be mentioned that in some countries these enforcing bodies do much more than just monitor compliance with environmental legislation and assist the police with technical expertise. When violations have been established, in some cases administrative enforcing bodies are able to impose administrative sanctions of various kinds themselves. This obviously raises questions with respect to co-ordination with the criminal prosecution, which will be considered briefly below.

Before addressing the role of victims in the criminal process in greater detail, it should again be mentioned that the administrative enforcing bodies could play various roles in the enforcement of environmental legislation. First, it was mentioned above that they could play an important role at the beginning of the enforcement procedure through their powers to inspect. Using their powers to inspect, they are usually the first to notice that a violation of environmental legislation has taken place. Second, in some cases enforcing bodies can apply administrative sanctions. These bodies should, however, not always necessarily be the same as the ones who exercise control. Taking into account the principle that investigation and sanctioning should preferably not be in the hands of the same organ, it might be better to have various instances deciding on inspection on the one hand and on eventual administrative sanctioning on the other. Administrative penalties will be further discussed below under section 4. In this respect it is, however, important to note that many countries, such as for instance Austria and Germany, know a specific administrative penalty procedure. The treatment as far as the preliminary investigation in both systems is the same, as the Austrian report states, but the substantive prerequisites for responsibility and the sanctions to be imposed and the procedure of the administrative penalty procedure do of course differ from those of the criminal justice procedure. The possibility of imposing administrative sanctions of course raises interesting questions with respect to the relationship with the criminal prosecution that can be exercised by the public prosecutor. Obviously, most legal systems which have the possibility of imposing administrative sanctions have a form of *electa una via* rule, which means that the authorities must choose between an administrative sanction and a criminal penalty.[3] In Germany the administrative agency must refer the case to the public prosecutor if the commission of an environmental crime is suspected. A question that arises in that respect is whether the public prosecutor has some control over the decision to impose an administrative

3 Unless the goals are totally different.

sanction or initiate a criminal prosecution. Finally, one could of course discuss the effectiveness of administrative sanctions in their relationship with criminal penalties in general. It is for instance remarkable in this respect that the Dutch report mentions that the disadvantage of the administrative enforcement is that administrative enforcing bodies tend to initiate lengthy and excessive negotiations with the actor before effectively applying sanctions.

2.3 Role of individuals and NGOs

2.3.1 Influence of individuals on the criminal enforcement of environmental law: general

Turning now to the role of individual citizens or NGOs in criminal law enforcement, the country reports indicate that these can have a different influence. First, it is mentioned that individuals can contribute to the quality of environmental legislation by pointing to weaknesses in some parts of the legislation, which may lead to amendments at the political level. Generally, it is also argued that public awareness of environmental problems will have a positive impact on the attitude of the legislator to take action with respect to environmental protection. The actions of NGOs, pointing at the sensitivity of certain topics in the public opinion, can of course also encourage legislative action.

Secondly, with respect to the criminal process, almost all respondents note that individuals may report violations of environmental legislation to the police or to specific enforcing bodies. Individuals can indeed be considered as important 'watchdogs' and thus be a cornerstone, leading to the prosecution of environmental crimes. This role of individuals (and especially NGOs) in reporting environmental crime should not be underestimated, given the inherent limitations in the possibilities of detection by the police and enforcing bodies. Since these cannot be everywhere at all times, it is useful that citizens themselves also function in their role of watchdogs of the environment.

The question obviously arises as to whether this role of individuals can be taken further somehow. By reporting an environmental crime, individuals can indeed trigger a criminal investigation, but this will as such obviously not be a guarantee that the actor will also be brought to trial. Individuals can, however, in some Member States (for instance England and Wales) also take action themselves.

The third possibility for citizen involvement in the enforcement of environmental law is bringing a civil law suit, claiming injunctive relief or compensatory damages. If the conditions of the environmental liability in the Member

States are met, in that particular case the individual will act as victim of environmental damage and will then commence an action in the civil courts, using the civil law system (usually tort law). Also the administrative body may be included in this action.

A fourth possibility would be that victims have the option of bringing their civil claim directly before a criminal court, thereby starting the criminal prosecution as well. This is only possible in specific Member States and will be discussed further below.

But even if individuals do not have the option of commencing a criminal prosecution themselves, they can usually still be involved in the criminal prosecution brought by the public prosecutor. This involvement can consist in providing help to the public prosecutor by either providing evidence or acting as a witness. This is specifically mentioned in the Italian report. As mentioned, a victim of an environmental offence may, with certain rights, participate in the proceedings, and has a right to appeal a decision of the prosecutor not to prosecute. Another possibility is that sometimes the civil law suit can still (within certain conditions) be brought before the criminal court once the public prosecutor has started the criminal prosecution. Under such circumstances, it is still the public prosecutor who will have started the proceedings, which may then be joined by the victim who can bring his or her civil suit to the criminal court.

2.3.2 The right to start a prosecution before the criminal court

A fundamental question in criminal procedure, which obviously also plays a role in the criminal enforcement of environmental law, is whether criminal prosecution is the monopoly of the public prosecutor. In a number of countries, as was indicated in the table, this is apparently the case. In Denmark, Germany, Italy, the Netherlands and Portugal, the public prosecutor is in principle the only authority competent to bring a criminal prosecution before the criminal court.

In some other countries, individuals can bring actions for environmental offences before a criminal court. This seems to be the case in Austria, Finland, Portugal and Spain. Although the question was formulated in such a way as to ask whether individuals can bring criminal prosecutions for environmental offences, it is not clear whether in the countries mentioned it is indeed the criminal prosecution which is brought by the individual. In some other countries, Belgium and France, for example, victims also have a right to bring an action against an offender in a criminal court, but in fact the individual in such cases is not applying the public action, but is simply bringing his or her civil law suit before the criminal court. In England and Wales, the

Environment Agency is the prosecuting body and individuals (including NGOs) have the right to bring a prosecution regardless of harm to themselves. Some cases will be referred to the Attorney General who decides whether it is in the public interest. The countries which allow individuals to bring a prosecution for environmental offences before the criminal court apparently grant this right to the individual if he or she can claim that he or she has been a victim. This is stressed in particular in the Finnish and Spanish country reports. It is important, since it shows that the reason that the individual can bring his or her claim to the criminal court is that he or she has been a victim. Usually those countries require that the individual must have suffered personal harm. As far as environmental cases are concerned, this can for example be the case if one was owner of a site or property which has been polluted by a third party. Still, if the individual is only bringing a claim as a victim, this is remarkably different from the situation where all individuals and NGOs have the right to initiate the criminal prosecution for environmental offences, even if they were not victims. In the latter case, individuals or NGOs would almost be acting in the public interest and bringing an *actio popularis*. That would obviously still go further than just bringing a claim as a victim. The Austrian report seems to indicate that such an *actio popularis* would be allowed in Austria and also the country report from Portugal seems to indicate that not only individuals, but also NGOs could bring criminal prosecutions for environmental offences.

If individuals have the right to bring a criminal prosecution, this raises the question of whether there should be co-ordination with the criminal prosecution by the public prosecutor. In that respect, the country report from Finland indicates that individuals or enforcing bodies do have the right to bring a criminal prosecution on their own and do not require prior authorization from the public prosecutor, but they do have to wait for the decision of the public prosecutor. This indicates that only when the public prosecutor decides not to prosecute can individuals and enforcing bodies do so. Also, other countries have options for individuals to react against non-prosecution by the public prosecutor. For instance, in Belgium and France, victims can represent themselves as 'civil parties' and bring a direct lawsuit before the criminal court, notwithstanding the decision of the public prosecutor. In the Netherlands, victims can complain against non-prosecution through the court of appeal.

It is striking that all country reports mention that although certain bodies and individuals can bring criminal prosecution for environmental offences, the role of the public prosecutor will not be affected (see the answers to question 2(f)).

Those countries that do not allow victims to bring a direct suit against the offender before a criminal court, sometimes still provide for the possibility that the victim may join the prosecution with his or her civil claim. In the Netherlands and in Denmark, victims still can claim compensation during the criminal procedure, although the jurisdiction to bring criminal prosecutions still lies with the public prosecutor.

In that respect, the answers from the country reports show that the situation of victims of environmental crimes does not differ substantially from that of other victims, as far as their procedural position is concerned. When a country allows a victim to bring direct suits against an offender before the criminal court, it usually applies to environmental crimes as well.

2.4 Summary and international perspective

Summarizing, one can say that the role of individuals is apparently important, most of all in providing information on environmental offences. They can often actually start the preliminary investigation by reporting the crime. Some countries allow for an even more active role for the victim, especially in cases where criminal prosecution is not the sole jurisdiction of the public prosecutor. In other cases, victims may join the action of the public prosecutor.

Also, the public enforcing bodies were revealed to be very important because of their expertise, which is of essential importance in proving infringements of licensing conditions, for example. Still, with the exception of England and Wales, the role of enforcing bodies seems to be limited to the preliminary investigation. The public prosecutor brings prosecutions before the court; when public enforcing bodies play a part before the criminal court, it is usually as witness. In cases of administrative offences, the competent administrative authority still has certain rights of participation if such cases are assumed by the prosecutor. In some cases, enforcing bodies might also have suffered personal harm and could then claim compensation as a victim in those legal systems where victims are allowed to bring legal actions or participate in the criminal proceedings.

Looking at these issues of the role of enforcing bodies and individuals in connection with environmental offences in a broader context, one could also examine whether the Convention of the Council of Europe or the AIDP resolutions mention anything specific in this respect. It is astonishing that the Convention of the Council of Europe[4] does not generally state that victims should have a right to intervene in the criminal procedure to claim compensa-

4 See Annex 3 to this report.

tion, for instance. This is also understandable. It is connected with the national criminal procedure in such a way that it could be almost impossible to constitute a common opinion in that respect. A provision which is of importance for this topic is Article 11, on the rights for groups to participate in proceedings. This Article merely provides that 'each party may, at any time, in a declaration, addressed to the secretary-general of the Council of Europe, declare that it will, in accordance with national law, grant any group, foundation or association which, according to its statutes, aims at the protection of the environment the right to participate in proceedings concerning environmental offences established in accordance with this convention'. Hence, there is no general duty for signatory States to introduce a right of NGOs to participate in proceedings, but signatory States may introduce this. It will obviously be most likely that countries where individuals already have the right to intervene in criminal proceedings, will introduce this provision.

There is one other provision of the Council of Europe Convention which is worth mentioning here, that being Article 10, which relates to co-operation between authorities. It provides:

> Cooperation between authorities
>
> 1. Each Party shall adopt such appropriate measures as may be necessary to ensure that the authorities responsible for environmental protection cooperate with the authorities responsible for investigating and prosecuting criminal offences:
>   (a) by informing the latter authorities, on their own initiative, where there are reasonable grounds to believe that an offence under Article 2 has been committed;
>   (b) by providing, upon request all necessary information, to the latter authorities, in accordance with domestic law.
> 2. Each Party may, at the time of signature or when depositing its instrument of ratification, acceptance, approval or accession, by a declaration addressed to the Secretary General of the Council of Europe, declare that it reserves the right not to apply paragraph 1 a of this Article or that it applies only to offences specified in such declaration.

This article, thus, apparently stresses the need for some co-operation between administrative agencies and criminal prosecution authorities, although it obviously remains difficult to regulate 'good cooperation' via legal texts.

The resolutions of the AIDP congress relate mostly to substantive environmental criminal law and do not have many specific provisions with respect to the right of individuals, NGOs or enforcing bodies to intervene in the criminal procedure.[5] One should point, however, to Resolution 24, which provides:

> Within the framework of the constitution and the basic law of national legal systems, legislation should facilitate the participation of citizens in the initiation of investigation and prosecution of alleged crimes against the environment.

3. CRIMINAL PENALTIES

3.1 Sanctions in environmental legislation

From the overview of the country reports, it appeared that most legal systems have a variety of criminal sanctions which can in theory be applied to environmental offences. Indeed, most of the traditional sanctions, imprisonment and fines, can be found in environmental law, either in specific provisions in the criminal codes aiming at the protection of ecological values, or in administrative legislation on environmental law. The most common sanctions are still, according to most respondents, imprisonment and fines. In that respect, environmental criminal law does not seem to differ much from the general field of criminal law. Of course, the severity of the punishment may well vary. In some of the more developped systems, a more or less elaborated variety of sanctions can be found which corresponds with the severity of the environmental crime. One would indeed expect that when not only administrative duties are violated (in the so-called abstract endangerment type of crimes) but also ecological values are directly infringed (in the concrete endangerment type of crimes) more severe penalties would pose a threat. This is sometimes, but not always, the case.[6] In cases of illegal disposal of dangerous waste, imprisonment is even imposed in practice (e.g., in Germany). Moreover, there may also be differences as far as the severity of penalties is concerned, depending on whether the criminal sanctions can be found in merely administrative laws or in the criminal codes themselves. Generally, but again this is not always the case, one can expect more severe sanctions in those legal systems where infringements of ecological values have been criminalized directly in a penal code; this is, however, not the case in Germany. In

5 See Annex 4 to this report.

6 An analysis of this has been made by Faure, M. and Visser, M., 'How to Punish Environmental Pollution? Some Reflections on Various Models of Criminalization of Environmental Harm', *European Journal of Crime, Criminal Law and Criminal Justice*, 1995, 316–368.

hat case, we can refer to the various overviews which have analyzed differences in substantive environmental criminal law. When only looking at the legislative framework that provides for the sanctions which can be applied in theory, one generally notices that the prison sanctions that are provided for violations of environmental law are generally less severe compared with sanctions provided by the penal code. This of course raises questions with respect to the possibility of these provisions offering adequate protection for ecological values. Still, in many countries (especially in those where environmental criminal law has not been incorporated into the penal code), one notices that infringements on traditional individual values (such as for instance life, health, property or honour) are still punished with more severe sanctions than infringements on collective values such as ecological interests.

The country reports all note that fines can be applied to the violation of environmental legislation, although some countries (e.g., Austria, Finland and Germany) have a specific system of so-called day fines. These are (see, e.g., the Finnish report) imposed as a certain number of days at a certain sum each day. The amount of the sum then ultimately depends on the monthly income and assets of the offender. This day fine system hence allows for some redistribution by taking into account each offender's individual income situation.[7]

3.2 Tendency towards low fines in practice

When we then turn to legal practice and see how, according to the various respondents, the legislative provisions are used in practice, we note that the fine is the criminal penalty most commonly used in legal practice. It is striking to note that not only is the fine apparently the most popular sanction, but that also the amounts imposed are on average relatively low. This seems to be true in all countries, with the exception of the Netherlands where the country report notes that fines of several hundred thousand guilders were actually imposed in serious cases and in Germany where sometimes prison sentences were imposed in the most serious cases.

Also this finding, that fines for environmental crimes are on average relatively low, corresponds with the literature. Several scholars have looked for

---

[7] This day-fine system has been well received by law and economics scholars who argue that the advantage of this system is that the available assets of the offender are used to an optimal amount. Hence, monetary sanctions (fines) can be used intensively without the necessity to use the costly prison sanction. See e.g. Cooter, R. and Ulen, Th., *Law and economics*, 3e edition, 2000, 451 and 471–472.

sources of these low fines and have criticized the attitude of courts in this respect. One source of the criticism is that the criminal sanction would not be able to fulfil its preventive function if only these low fines were to be imposed. It has indeed been argued that, especially in cases of environmental crime where corporate offenders may play a considerable role, the hypothesis of the rational, calculating criminal is a realistic one. In that respect, it must not be forgotten that often significant financial investments have to be made to comply with environmental legislation. Hence, there can be a substantial material gain from violating environmental law (for instance, by not having to invest in a water-cleaning installation or other abatement technology). Assuming that incentives for adopting this kind of technology would only come from the criminal law,[8] the sanction should take into account the low probability of detection. Therefore, the sanction should be a multiple of the potential benefit to the criminal to outweigh the low detection rate. If this were not the case, a rational, calculating offender would, assuming risk neutrality, prefer to violate environmental law. These findings show that from a criminal policy perspective, one can improve compliance by either improving the detection rate or increasing the expected penalty. Since increasing the detection rate is much more costly, policy-makers often choose to increase the expected penalty,[9] which must then be great enough to account for the relatively low detection rate.

However, when fines are applied, one should also take into account that at a certain level potential offenders will no longer be deterred by fines, given the insolvency risk. This may occur as soon as the potential magnitude of the fine exceeds the potential offenders wealth.[10] Threatening the offender with a fine exceeding his wealth will obviously not prove to be an effective deterrent. For that reason in particular, in the literature the use of non-monetary sanctions has been advocated in cases where there might be a risk of insolvency.[11] A well-known non-monetary sanction is of course imprisonment. Legal practice apparently reveals that imprisonment is rarely used or only used if the

---

8 Which is of course not true in practice: other (financial) incentives such as the tax system and administrative coercive measures may well play an important role as well.

9 See Polinsky, M. and Shavell, S., 'A note on optimal fines when wealth varies among individuals', *American Economic Review*, 1991, vol. 81, 618.

10 See Polinsky, A.M. and Shavell, S., 'The optimal trade off between the probability and the magnitude of fines', *American Economic Review*, 1979, 880–891.

11 See Shavell, S., 'Criminal law and the optimal use of non-monetary sanctions as a deterrent', *Columbia Law Review*, 1985, 1232–1262 and Coffee, J.C., 'Corporate crime and punishment. A non-Chicago view of the economics of criminal sanctions', *American Criminal Law Review*, 1980, 419–476.

fines are not paid. In those cases where prison sanctions are imposed, they are relatively low on average (compared to common crimes) and often suspended on probation. This once more corresponds with the general finding in the literature on environmental criminal law that prison sanctions are almost never used.[12]

3.3 Alternative criminal penalties

At a normative level, one could at first blush argue that the enforcement of criminal law is therefore largely ineffective, since the economic analysis we just provided predicts that some offenders can only be deterred (because of the insolvency risk) through non-monetary sanctions. This conclusion should however be balanced. First of all, we should always take into account the fact that in no legal system is environmental criminal law the only legal instrument to deter environmental pollution. Criminal law is usually (and, in the opinion of the authors, rightly) used as a last resort and in combination with many other (administrative, financial and civil) legal instruments. When a modest prison sanction is indeed used as a last resort in combination with a number of other instruments, this might well be effective. Moreover, in some cases the suspension on probation of a prison sanction might well prove to be highly effective, for example, in compelling corporate managers to invest in abatement technology which they may previously have refused to do. The threat of otherwise having to go to jail, even if this were for just a short time, might well give the appropriate incentives to these 'white-collar criminals'.

Moreover, as mentioned above (see generally question 1), real environmental crime typically is corporate crime, especially in the more serious cases. Although it was argued that the individual responsibility of officers, directors and managers remains of crucial importance, it is equally important to provide for adequate reactions against collective failure. Obviously, prison sanctions cannot fulfil this role. If, therefore, other corporate sanctions could be applied which effectively deter environmental crime, the relatively low prison sanctions should as such not be a problem.

However, also in this respect the results from the country reports are disappointing. Direct sanctions and measures aimed at environmental

---

12 See Heine, G., 'Environmental criminality and its control', in Eser, A. and Thormundsson, J. (eds.), *Old ways and new needs in criminal legislation*, Freiburg im Breisgau, Max Planck Institute for foreign and international criminal law, 1989, 255–279.

restoration or prevention of future harm seem to be rarely applied in practice.[13] Only some countries (especially Denmark and Sweden, and sometimes, though rarely, Germany) confiscate the illegal gains in environmental cases.[14] This obviously raises the question as to how the financial benefit of an environmental crime should be defined, a question which is greatly debated in the literature. Obviously financial incentives other than criminal or administrative fines can be imposed as well to give incentives to comply with environmental law. Economic incentives such as levies and taxes are well-known methods to correct environmental pollution but a discussion of their importance would be beyond the scope of this report.

Other sanctions which could be applied according to legislation, such as for instance the shutdown of a specific installation, are apparently almost never applied in practice in criminal law. This seems to be problematic since it has rightly been argued in the literature that specifically these direct sanctions and measures can be very effective in controlling environmental crime, more specifically in the corporate sphere.

Is the conclusion then that it follows from the country reports that the criminal penalties are too weak for environmental criminal law to be effective? Of course, it is not possible within the scope of this report to make a general judgement on the effectiveness of the criminal law, since this would require a much more in-depth analysis. Nevertheless, it should be stressed that the mere fact that criminal penalties are indeed relatively weak (based on the low average) should not generally lead to an overall negative conclusion, as far as applying criminal law to environmental issues is concerned. The country reports also indicate some reasons for the preferences for fines and the relatively low average of criminal penalties. One main reason is the fact that most offences are minor and the offenders are often first-time offenders. In addition, the Dutch country report properly mentions that in some cases criminal penalties are relatively low for the simple reason that an administrative sanction has already been applied. Indeed, not all countries consider as a general rule that the application of an administrative sanction excludes the application of the criminal law. Sometimes the mere threat of criminal sanctions can be an effective deterrent to environmental crime, even in cases where the sanctions imposed are relatively low. Hence, one cannot judge the

---

13 Recent evolutions show that the removal of illegal gain is now also applied in Belgium and the Netherland, also in environmental cases.

14 See on the removal of illegal gain in environmental cases in Germany Franzheim, H., 'Der Verfall des Vermögensvorteils in Umweltstrafsachen – sein Umfang und seine Berechnung', *Wistra*, 1989, 87–90 and Franzheim, H., 'Gewinnabschöpfung im Umweltstrafrecht', *Wistra*, 1986, 253–255.

effectiveness of an environmental criminal justice system just by considering the average level of sanctions imposed. Moreover, one should take into account that often during the negotiation phase the threat of sanctions may be used to coerce offenders to comply with environmental legislation or to solve the problem they have caused. These negotiations can take place through various authorities. Negotiations will typically be the instrument used by administrative authorities, but some countries also allow the public prosecutor to 'bargain' in some respect with the offender by forcing him or her for instance to repair the harm done. In some cases, the public prosecutor might (explicitly or implicitly) reward the offender who actually repaired the harm done by either not prosecuting at all or by imposing a lower penalty than the statutory maximum. This negotiation and bargaining approach is obviously not possible within all legal systems and, at first sight, does not fit into the deterrence model of criminal law. However, in particular cases this approach may well be effective if it comes to solving the environmental problem at hand.[15] This should also be taken into account if one looks at the relatively low average. If, as a consequence of bargaining with the administrative authorities or the public prosecutor, the offender invested in the required abatement technology or repaired the harm done, then the approach to impose only a relatively modest fine for the initial wrongdoing should not necessarily be bad. But again, this thinking fits more into an *ex post* approach to the environmental problem, whereby the threat of criminal sanctions is used to solve the problem after it has occurred; from an *ex ante* deterrence point of view, the mere fact that problems have been solved afterwards should not be a reason to impose lower sanctions, given the potential benefits of infringing the law on the one hand and the low detection rate with the low risks of imposition of a sanction on the other. Nevertheless, some legislators, such as those of the Netherlands and the UK, have adopted these possibilities and in other countries the practice looks for adequate ways to deal with complex matters that differ from traditional criminal law.

3.4 Reasons for low sanctions in environmental legal practice

Of course there are also reasons for imposing relatively low sanctions, which cannot be explained by the reasons mentioned above. Still, in many countries the judiciaries' lack of familiarity with environmental law, for instance because it is still a relatively new field, might be one of the reasons why the moral blame for these kind of offences is not felt as being very strong, which

---

15 See on the efficiency of plea bargaining.

might also account for the low sanctions. To this can be added the fact that in some countries public awareness of the harmful consequences of environmental crime might still be low. Sometimes the judges do not consider environmental crimes as very damaging to society for the simple fact that in some countries environmental crimes have not been introduced in the criminal code, so that even a case of serious water pollution is merely punished as an infringement of provisions of an administrative licence. If this case is then merely considered as one in which administrative provisions were breached and no attention is given to the fact that with this breach serious harm was caused to ecological values, one can understand that the prosecution of such a case will not lead to imposing high sanctions.

In some cases, the fact that the offenders in environmental criminal cases who will appear in court are not the traditional 'outcasts' or the usual subject of criminal law but rather are the directors or managers of highly respected firms may play a role as well. This is of course the traditional problem when prosecuting white-collar crime, which might even play a more significant role in environmental cases. Some of the traditional judicial actions against white-collar criminals were directed towards the 'losers' in the business society, who went bankrupt or cheated the normal rules of market competition, for example. But in the case of environmental law, often the successful businessmen and entrepreneurs are also confronted with criminal prosecution. This, together with the impact of the socio-economic interest of the particular firm at issue (e.g., employing a high number of persons), might make clear why in many countries courts are still relatively reluctant to impose high, deterrent sanctions on environmental crime.

It is also striking to note that with few exceptions (for instance Denmark and the UK) the possibilities of imposing corporate sanctions are not used frequently, although this does not mean that criminal prosecutions would not be directed against corporations. In legal systems that accept corporate liability one will notice that prosecutions are indeed primarily directed at companies and only at employees (such as managers) in case of intentional wrongdoing. Here, reference is made to the fact that sanctions which are primarily directed at controlling corporate crime (such as for instance restoration orders or confiscation of illegal gain) are infrequently used in practice (again England and Wales seem to be exceptions). This is striking since, as it was indicated above (see question 1), environmental crime is typically (in the more serious cases) corporate crime, to which the criminal justice system should adapt itself, not only by looking at possibilities of collective responsibility, but also in providing an adequate sanctioning system. Apparently, sanctions which are typically directed at enterprises (such as repairing harm done, shutting down an illegal installation, publishing a judgement) are only rarely used. They are not even used in systems which have an elaborate choice of corporate sanctions (as is the case in the Dutch economic crimes act) and not even in systems which have the collective responsibility of legal entities (as in the Netherlands).[16] In some legal systems there is only a tendency to pronounce the confiscation of illegal gain.

Usually, prison sanctions or fines are still applied (if at all). The only notable issue is that, in cases of corporate environmental crime, in some countries the fines are considerably higher. This might explain why in the Netherlands sanctions of up to a million guilders (today approximately 450,000 euro) were sometimes imposed as a fine. The reason these corporate sanctions are not applied is that they are apparently considered too heavy for the defendant or, more importantly, that execution requires the co-operation of administrative enforcing bodies. Indeed, if the public prosecutor requires and the judge imposes the sanction of repairing harm done, the public prosecutor will often not have the traditional means of execution to verify how such a judgement is actually enforced. The actual co-operation between administrative authorities and the public prosecutor or the judge as far as the enforcement of those direct measures is concerned might require a more specific regulation, as is available in England and Wales. For instance, ordering the removal of illegally deposited waste will have little effect if the same measures have already been ordered before by way of an administrative measure and have not been executed. Sometimes imposing a penalty payment can be used in case of non-compliance, but this will have little effect if the offender is insolvent or out of reach. This insolvency problem also arises for example when an order to repay decontamination costs has been issued. In some cases direct sanctions might not be necessary any longer, especially in those where the offender has meanwhile complied with the administrative requirements. In those cases one can understand that only a fine is imposed once the violation has been undone as a result of the pressure of criminal prosecution.

3.5 Who imposes criminal sanctions?

All country reports stated that the criminal sanctions are imposed by the courts. There is obviously a whole range of other sanctions which can be imposed, but those which qualify as *criminal* penalties can only be imposed

---

16 Although it should be also stressed that legal systems which do not accept the criminal liability of legal entities sometimes do have sanctions which can be directed towards entities.

by a court. Some legal systems have created regimes of administrative penalties, which were discussed in relation to question 4. Some countries (such as Italy, Portugal and Germany) have specific regimes for administrative offences (the so-called 'Ordnungswidrigkeiten'), with administrative fines as the main form of sanction.

In addition, reference should again be made to the possibilities which exist in some legal systems for the public prosecutor to abstain from prosecution, provided that the offender meets specific conditions. This can also include paying a fine. In some countries, such as the Netherlands, the public prosecutor may 'settle' some of the environmental criminal cases against the payment of substantial fines by the offender. In most environmental cases, a so-called 'transaction' is offered to the offender. It usually concerns smaller cases, but can also sometimes involve larger cases. This practice of imposing high monetary sanctions, even for serious environmental crimes, is, however, the subject of a great deal of debate in literature. Given the uncertainty of a trial, one may well argue that this practice is effective from the point of view of the public prosecutor and that it might have some deterrent effect, especially if a fine is imposed in combination with a duty to repair harm done. There is also the advantage for the offender of avoiding a public criminal trial by complying with the conditions set by the public prosecutor. The criticism against this practice is that when these amounts of fines are imposed, the environmental crimes are sometimes of a more serious nature and should normally not be settled out of court, but rather should be prosecuted. Another criticism is that through this practice some of the more serious environmental crimes are never prosecuted and therefore remain hidden from the open public debate that takes place during a hearing before the criminal court. Hence, some of the general preventive effect of a court hearing would be lost.[17]

3.6 International perspective

In this evaluation, this section can be concluded with a brief look at the attitude of the Convention of the Council of Europe and the AIDP congress recommendations to compare them with actual legal practice in Europe as far as criminal penalties is concerned. The Council of Europe Convention on the Protection of the Environment through Criminal Law[18] provides in Article 6 that 'each party shall adopt, in accordance with the relevant international

[17] Although it must be mentioned that some of the settlements with the public ministry leading to the payment of very high fines by the offender also received the necessary publicity.

[18] See Annex 3 to this report.

instruments, such appropriate measures as may be necessary to enable it to make the offences established in accordance with Articles 2 and 3 [intentional and negligent serious offences] punishable by criminal sanctions which take into account the serious nature of these offences. The sanctions available shall include imprisonment and pecuniary sanctions and may include reinstatement of the environment.'

This provision apparently requires that the offences should be made punishable by criminal sanctions; this appears to exclude the possibility that some of these serious offences which harm ecological values and cause specific risks would only be punished with administrative fines (Article 4 deals with administrative offences). This refers to abstract endangerment offences such as the unlawful discharge without further requirements with respect to the nature of the pollution. Thus, if the offence consists of a mere administrative violation (e.g. violation of licence conditions), here administrative penalties may be applied. Moreover, the criminal penalties should also take into account the serious nature of these offences. As far as the nature of the sanctions is concerned, Article 6 provides that these shall include imprisonment and pecuniary sanctions, which is, as is illustrated in the table, apparently already the case in most of the countries today.

As far as direct or corporate sanctions are concerned, Article 6 only states that the sanctions may include reinstatement of the environment. The reinstatement order is further developed in Article 8. However, introduction of this measure is apparently not mandatory for the signatory States. Article 7 further provides that all parties agree to 'adopt measures to confiscate instrumentalities and proceeds or property, the value of which corresponds to such proceeds'. Hence, some form of removal of the illegal gain should also be introduced.[19]

Turning to the resolutions of the XVth international congress of penal law of the AIDP,[20] point 7 of the resolutions states that a distinction should be drawn between sanctions which are imposed for non-observance of established administrative and regulatory standards, which do not include deprivation of liberty or punitive closing of an enterprise, and criminal sanctions which are imposed to prevent and punish culpable acts or omissions that cause serious harm to the environment. Until now, not all the countries under consideration take this distinction into account.

---

[19] See on the efficiency of the removal of illegal gain Bowles, R., Faure, M. and Garoupa, N., 'Economic analysis of the removal of illegal gains', *International Review of Law and Economics*, 2000, vol. 20, 537–549.

[20] Included in Annex 4 to this report.

4. ADMINISTRATIVE SANCTIONS

Establishing a side system to criminal law, which allows different kinds of repressive sanctions by administrative bodies is a European-wide tendency. For instance in Denmark and the Netherlands, there is an ongoing discussion to extend the possibilities of administrative bodies influencing behaviour to ensure compliance with regulations. All other member parties (with the exception of England and Wales)[21] have well-established systems of administrative fines, imposed by administrative bodies. However, in some countries it has been well-documented by more profound research that there has been a kind of 'civil-war' between the criminal prosecutor and the administrative agency in respect of the adequate kind of reaction in the case of environmental pollution. In no way should the speedy reaction allowed by administrative sanctions be underestimated, mostly on a procedure based on lower standards.[22] However, in respect of the important principle of co-operation between administrative agency and enterprise, it should be clarified that a differentiation should be legally established between the different competences of administrative agencies (to grant a permission, to manage and impose administrative penal sanctions). Furthermore, in many countries there is a need for obligations imposed on administrative agencies to inform the prosecutor about most serious cases of pollution. In Germany, a legal duty provides that the case must be referred to the prosecutor if the commission of a criminal offence is suspected. The same is the case in other countries such as Belgium. This means that administrative authorities lose the discretion to settle the case once a criminal offence is suspected. In those situations, the case must be referred to the public prosecutor. However, the principle of co-operation at the administrative level seems to result in the administrative bodies trying to cover up the case for as long as possible. Indeed, administrative authorities seem to attach more credence to co-operation leading an offender to compliance than to deterrence through application of the criminal law. In practice therefore only intrinsic and persistent polluters are reported to the prosecutor.

However, this is no argument against the importance of these side systems. Furthermore, administrative criminal sanctions are very specific in respect of

---

21 Criticism of the lack of administrative sanctions is formulated by Ogus, A. and Abbot, C., 'Sanctions for pollution: do we have the right regime?', *Journal of Environmental Law*, 2002, vol. 14, 283–300.

22 The effectiveness of administrative sanctions and their comparison to criminal penalties is also discussed in § 8 A of this chapter.

their specific objectives, namely strengthening compliance with administrative orders and a quick and adequate solution for obvious infringements of administrative regulations without further consequences (i.e. damage). These are the so-called technical breaches.

Most countries within their systems have properly differentiated between the 'real' hard-core criminal law[23] and these side systems in respect of the material prerequisites and the procedure.[24] As a rule, they have (formally or in practice) relaxed the classical principles of criminal law and further relaxed the procedural requirements, especially with respect to evidence and possibilities to appeal to a higher court. In any case, the offender must still be able (as it is established in all countries) to go to a court. Corresponding to the national tradition, the administrative sanction, its prerequisites and its procedure are in some cases more strongly influenced by criminal law, and in some cases more by administrative methods. Even in an ever-expanding Europe, these national traditions should be preserved if they ensure minimum standards of due process. Finally, the legislators have a wide discretion as regards which cases of environmental pollution should be treated by criminal law or by these repressive side systems.

5. EXISTENCE OF INSTRUMENTS WHICH PROHIBIT INDIVIDUALS FROM CARRYING OUT A SIMILAR ACTIVITY

5.1 General issue

Bearing in mind the general trend of European legislations, namely broadeningthe spectrum of sanctions, prohibition orders could play a prominent role in the protection of the environment. Some countries have a long tradition with these sanctions, others have merely had some recent experience. Taking the historical development of prohibition orders into consideration, their place of birth is administrative law, but some countries have also incorporated these measures into the criminal code as criminal sanctions. However, many countries are reluctant to incorporate these sanctions into the criminal regime. There may be a correlation between the newness of these sanctions given to the criminal court and the fact that this measure is so seldom imposed in practice. However, having a look at the typical offender in criminal law in many countries (farmers, small business operators, first-time

23 In Germany, this is referred to as 'Kernstrafrecht'.

24 This system for administrative offences is in Germany referred to as 'Ordnungswidrigkeitsrecht'.

offenders), it is clear that in many cases the legal prerequisites for prohibiting carrying out a similar activity are not fulfilled. Furthermore, one should take into consideration that it is usually the criminal court and not the prosecutor who imposes the formal prohibition order. Nevertheless, the typical final decision in an environmental criminal case in many countries, especially if large-scale enterprises are involved, is the discontinuance of the case under certain conditions. To these conditions belong, for example, restoration, forfeiture or investments in improving risk balancing of the enterprise, but not a personal prohibition order. A personal prohibition order generally causes problems from a constitutional perspective. Most countries provide for special safeguards of the profession, which cannot simply be removed during this early stage of the criminal procedure. A prohibition order directed against a person usually at least requires a decision of a criminal court.

However, prohibition notices imposed not on individuals but on legal entities play an important role in the UK.

5.2 Specific questions

An ongoing problem in the Member States seems to be an individual (sentenced by a prohibition order) operating undercover for another company. Many reasons might explain this result. First, these cases are hard to detect. Furthermore, a possible increase in controlling activities of entities legally run has no relationship with possible results. Finally, sufficient suspicion is another requirement in respect of illegal activities. Therefore, a possible solution could be the legal route taken by the United Kingdom. The administrative body serves the prohibition notice on the body corporate which stops operation of a particular plant. It is site specific. It is a crime (in continental European systems preferable: a contravention or an administrative offence) to contravene the prohibition order. It seems to be more effective to focus the prohibition orders on specific serious cases committed by organizations. Taking into consideration that serious cases of environmental pollution very often are not the result of a single decision but more of a wrongful development over a period of time, it seems to be preferable to impose the prohibition orders on corporations as such, but which might also be done by administrative authorities. Therefore, one can effectively see the problem that serious cases are often indicators of a criminal corporate culture, which means an attitude, policy, rule, cause of conduct or practice existing within the body corporate generally.[25]

---

[25] See Heine, G., Die strafrechtliche Verantwortlichkeit von Unternehmen. Von individuellem Fehlverhalten zu kollektiven Fehlentwicklungen, insbesondere bei Großrisiken, Baden-Baden, Nomos, 1995.

6. TRANSFRONTIER POLLUTION INCIDENTS

6.1 Examples

Some countries report having little or no problems with transfrontier pollution incidents (UK, Spain). This may be partially due to their location (which could be the case for the UK); in other countries there is a potential for transfrontier pollution incidents (for instance between Portugal and Spain), but no particular report of problems is made. However, the Portuguese respondent reports problems of marine oil pollution on the Atlantic coast of Portugal, caused by oil tankers illegally washing tanks.[26] Most countries which report transfrontier pollution incidents mention that it concerns cases of transboundary water pollution, usually involving transboundary rivers. This apparently is the case for Austria and Finland. Some countries in addition report problems with water pollution incidents which take place just outside the territorial waters. This was also the case for Finland, where 100 cases of marine oil pollution were reported in 1997 and with Italy, where report is made of a spectacular case of the sinking of 80 ships with radioactive waste.

Other countries, such as Germany and the Netherlands, report that their cases of transfrontier pollution incidents concern mainly cases of waste transport, nuclear materials and import of endangered species.[27]

In some of these cases, the facts made clear that the transboundary character of the pollution incident did not cause specific problems from the point of view of the criminal law. For instance, Austria reported that in a case of major water pollution between Austria and Slovenia, both countries started an investigation and prosecution. In that particular case, there could have been an issue as to which country had the right to continue the prosecution,[28] and

---

26 See generally on these problems Gold, E., *Handbook on marine pollution*, Gard, 1985 and especially concerning the recent incidents with the Erika and the Prestige: Le Couviour, K., 'Responsabilité pour pollutions majeures resultant du transport maritime d'hydrocarbure: après l'Erika, le Prestige … L'impératif de responsabilisation', *La Semaine Juridique (JCB)*, 18 December 2002, 2271.

27 The problems concerning transboundary transport of waste have been described by Lavrysen, L., 'Judicial responses in the nineties to Dutch (and German) shipments of waste to Belgium in the eithies', *Maastricht Journal of European and Comparative Law*, 1995, 219–234.

28 See on the international regime concerning the cooperation in the field of (environmental) criminal affairs Van der Wilt, H., 'Instruments of international cooperation in the field of criminal affairs', in Faure, M. and Heine, G., Environmental criminal law in the European Union, Max Planck Institute for foreign and international criminal law, Freiburg im Breisgau, 2000, 429–443.

it could have been investigated whether the *ne bis in idem* rule also applied in a transfrontier context. The Finnish river pollution case apparently posed no problems for the simple reason that the two directors who had polluted and were subsequently prosecuted and sentenced in Finland apparently were Finnish citizens, which also had negative consequences in Finland. This explains why in that particular case the transboundary character most likely did not pose any additional problems.[29]

In sum, transfrontier pollution in practice seems to follow the rule 'all or nothing'; that is, if there is transfrontier pollution, the resulting difficulties are enormous.

6.2 Specific 'transboundary' problems

In other cases, specific problems relating to the transboundary character of the pollution incident did indeed arise. It is striking that most of the problems mentioned in the country reports seem to be of a more practical nature and to have less to do with questions of substantive environmental law, such as whether the act constituted a crime in two legal systems. Some practical problems that are reported relate to the difficulty that, in cases of transboundary incidents, it might be necessary to hear a defendant in a neighbouring country. Some countries report that it is sometimes difficult to obtain essential information from neighbouring countries (Austria, the Netherlands). One example is an Italian case concerning the sinking of a ship with toxic waste where a Greek captain, who sailed back to Greece, was apparently suspected.There was no subsequent support from Greece in the investigation. In contrast, the Dutch report argues that generally co-operation between neighbouring States can be considered good.

In other cases, the specific problems relate not to a lack of co-operation of neighbouring States, but to the material problem that for instance in case of transboundary shipment of waste, organized crime is involved in a complex network of firms in different countries, which makes the investigation

---

29 The case might have been different if harmful consequences had only occurred in Russia and not in Finland. In that case, the wrongful act would have taken place in Finland, whereas the harmful effects would have taken place in Russia. Then, the question that becomes important is whether the criminal provision focuses on the wrongful emission or on the wrongful consequence. In the latter case, the competence of the Finnish court might be problematic. For further details on this issue, see e.g. Martin, J., *Strafbarkeit grenzüberschreitender Umweltbeeinträchtigungen. Zugleich ein Beitrag zur Gefährdungsdogmatik und zum Umweltvölkerrecht*, Max Planck Institute for foreign and international criminal law, Freiburg im Breisgau, 1989 and Wolswijk, H.D., *Locus delicti en rechtsmacht*, Deventer, Gouda Quint, 1998.

extremely difficult. In other cases, the problems do not so much relate to a lack of co-operation between neighbouring States, but to the fact that offences take place on the open sea, where no jurisdiction exists. For example, in Finland many cases of marine oil pollution were discovered through aeroplane surveillance. In those cases, Finland itself apparently lacks jurisdiction to act since the incidents take place outside their territorial waters, but offences can then be reported to the flag State. In this respect, Germany has established a wider extraterritorial jurisdiction.

Some of these above-mentioned problems relate only slightly to problems of substantive environmental criminal law, although it is interesting that these problems are apparently not considered a major issue in legal practice. This is interesting, since in legal doctrine and dogma a great deal of attention has been paid to how environmental criminal law should be shaped so that it may be applied in transboundary incidents, taking account the requirement of dual criminal liability and the applicable principles of criminal law.[30] From the responses of the country reporters, one gets the impression that these problems apparently only play a major role in legal doctrine, and not in practice. For instance, whether, in case of transboundary water pollution, the crimes should relate to the wrongful act (the emission) or to the wrongful effect (the pollution), since the latter can take place in another country. Another issue which is discussed a great deal in the literature is how one should deal with cases where an emission took place in compliance with a foreign licence.[31] Can such a foreign licence have a justificative effect? Apparently, all of these issues, however theoretically interesting they may be, do not play a major role in legal practice. Only the Dutch report refers directly to problems of substantive environmental criminal law by stating that a different policy towards environmental crime in other countries may affect the decision of the authorities to co-operate. This could be an argument for some kind of a unification of policies.

6.3 Effectiveness of existing treaties

Finally, the question was asked whether the existing formal treaties are considered sufficient to enable effective investigation and extradition. Once more,

---

30 Indeed, many international conventions require dual criminal liability. See the discussion by Van der Wilt, H., *l.c.*

31 See generally on the justificative effect of licences Rose-Ackerman, S., *Rethinking the progressive agenda. The reform of the American regulatory state*, 1992, 123 and Arcuri, A., 'Controlling environmental risk in Europe: the complementary role of an EC environmental liability regime', *Tijdschrift voor Milieuaansprakelijkheid*, 2001, 37–45.

it should be stated that the instruments of international co-operation in the field of criminal affairs were discussed in greater detail in a previous report.[32] Again, it is striking that in response to this question concerning the effectiveness of the existing treaties, the respondents only report practical problems relating to, for instance, exchange of information. Austria and Italy report that it is very difficult to get essential information, but no mention is made of the fact that the formal procedures would be applied, but only that requests would not have been answered. Also, in the Italian case with the Greek captain sailing back to Greece, whether Italy formulated a formal request for co-operation to the Greek authorities and what the response was remain unanswered. Finland mentioned a flaw in a formal treaty in its report. The flaw concerns the fact that the so-called Marpol convention (on marine oil pollution) does not provide for stopping a ship on the open sea.[33] Also the Belgian contribution sketches a number of problems concerning the effectiveness of existing treaties with respect to offences against the environment. It is noticed that there are unmistakable legal obstacles to prosecution of transboundary environmental crime. In addition, the Belgian respondent mentioned that in practice the available legal instruments are less often used in cases of cross-border offences against the environment than when other transboundary offences are committed (such as international drug trafficking). The reason for this is that, unlike in other cross-border matters, services such as interpol or the customs are not yet in the habit of, for instance, reporting an international waste transport to their foreign colleagues.

Nevertheless, the Netherlands, Germany and Portugal agree that there are enough bodies of international co-operation. The only question that arises is whether the existing instruments are indeed used satisfactorily. There may be a lack of knowledge with respect to the existing possibilities. The German rapporteur thus concludes that co-operation, and not necessarily organization, must be intensified. However, improvements of the European legal instruments on international co-operation in criminal matters are to be expected soon (extension of Schengen rules, amendments to the multilateral conventions of the Council of Europe on the level of the EU and the EC).

In international criminal law, usually the requirement of incrimination in both States is seen as a serious impediment for extradition. Interestingly enough, none of the respondents mentioned this requirement as being a problem. Hence, from the perspective of international co-operation, there is apparently no direct need for harmonization of environmental criminal law,

---

32 See Van der Wilt, H., *l.c.*

33 See Gold, E., *Handbook on marine pollution*, 58–74.

since the remaining differences between environmental criminal law in the Member States are not mentioned as a potential source of insufficient co-operation as far as the investigation of transboundary crime is concerned. In this respect, the authors of the European Convention on the Protection of the Environment through Criminal Law and those who recently took initiatives with respect to environmental criminal law at the European level may have a different opinion.

One should, however, be careful with this conclusion. The fact that many respondents state that they have not experienced any problems with the prosecution of transboundary environmental crime might simply mean that many of these cases are never actually prosecuted. During a workshop, it was indeed advanced that once major transboundary cases are actually investigated the legal problems that arise are much greater. The optimistic view offered in the country reports might therefore not be completely representative.

6.4 International perspective

Turning finally to the Convention of the Council of Europe and the AIDP resolutions, it should be mentioned that the Council of Europe convention[34] includes a number of provisions with respect to the measures to be taken at international level. For instance, Article 12(1) provides, with respect to international co-operation, that the parties 'shall afford each other, in accordance with the provisions of relevant international instruments on international co-operation in criminal matters and with their domestic law, the widest measure of co-operation in investigations and judicial proceedings relating to criminal offences established in accordance with this Convention'.

The AIDP resolutions[35] also have a number of specific provisions concerning jurisdiction and transboundary crime. Rule 25, for instance, provides that 'where the harm or serious risk of harm (*concrete endangerment*) that underlies a core crime against the environment arises outside the jurisdiction of a State where the crime is committed, wholly or in part, it should be possible […] to prosecute the accused in the State where the crime was committed, or in any State where the harm or serious risk of harm arises'. Rule 26 further provides that where the harm or serious risk of harm 'arises in the global commons, States should agree on an international convention or implement existing

34 See Annex 3 to this report.

35 Annex 4 to this report.

international conventions that would enable them to prosecute the crime by applying, in the following order:the flag principle;

- the principle of nationality;
- the principle of extradite or prosecute;

and, in cases of generally acknowledged international crimes, the principal of universality'.[36]

Of special importance is also Rule 23, which provides that 'core crimes against the environment affecting more than one national jurisdiction or affecting the global commons outside any national jurisdiction should be recognized as international crimes under multilateral conventions'.

7. CRIMINAL LIABILITY FOR ENVIRONMENTAL OFFENCES BY PUBLIC SERVANTS AND PUBLIC AUTHORITIES

7.1 General issues

Environmental criminal law is usually directed against the 'polluters'. However, legal doctrine in many countries has appropriately pointed to the fact that as a result of the so-called administrative dependence of environmental criminal law it is often the administrative authorities that determine the content of environmental criminal law. Hence, by being extremely lenient, that is, through the granting of flexible licences, the content of environmental criminal law could be substantially reduced. A consequence of this relationship between administrative and environmental criminal law is therefore that administrative authorities could through their negligence or wilful conduct substantially contribute to pollution caused by industry. Also, the extent to which environmental criminal law is effective depends to a large extent on controls exercised by administrative authorities. In some cases it is held that administrative authorities would be too flexible, that is, by providing no control at all or by giving the polluter the impression that his or her behaviour could in fact be lawful. Thus legal doctrine has held that administrative authorities sometimes substantially contribute to environmental offences. This has, therefore, more particularly in German legal doctrine, led to the question whether under specific circumstances civil servants or administrative authorities themselves should be held liable under the criminal

---

36 See further rules 27–29 of the AIDP resolutions, provided for in the annex 4.

law as well. This idea originated in Germany under the notion 'Amtsträgerstrafbarkeit'[37] but is meanwhile also largely discussed in other jurisdictions.

As a rule, all Member States provide criminal sanctions against public servants. However, the means used to prosecute civil servants can be divided in two categories. The first is characterized by the classic criminal provision 'abuse of administrative power'. These criminal provisions seem to have no practical importance. Several reasons are possible. One of the most important reasons may be that criminal liability occurs without any requirement of damage; the violation of administrative duties as such is a crime. However, criminological research has indicated social interferences between damage and the enforcement of criminal provisions. This means, for example, the great importance of the mass media reporting on damages to the environment. Newspapers and television influence the activities of prosecutors; investigations to detect a person responsible may lead to institutions 'behind' the direct polluter. Furthermore, the reports criticize the legal conditions imposing responsibility stating that they are very strict (Belgium). For that reason, other countries have used the second option of providing special provisions for illegal behaviour of civil servants causing pollution (Spain) or the courts have opened the door to imposing criminal sanctions on civil servants in the case of faulty decisions or faulty non-intervention (Germany, the Netherlands) indirectly causing pollution. In Portugal, following the German theory and practice, the doctrine developed criminal liability of civil servants in case of illegally damaging nature, or illegally polluting environmental components.

In some countries, such as the Netherlands, any pollution indirectly caused by an illegal act or omission of a civil servant can be criminally prosecuted.[38] In Germany, however, this occurs mainly in the area of water pollution and waste disposal. On the one hand, the German criminal code provides a broad spectrum of environmental crimes, such as polluting the water, the soil, the air, specific protected areas, illegal waste disposal, illegal operation of a

---

37 See e.g. Meinberg, V., 'Amtsträgerstrafbarkeit bei Umweltbehörden', *Neue Juristische Wochenschrift*, 1986, 2220–2228; Keller, R., 'Zur strafrechtlichen Verantwortlichkeit des Amtsträgers für fehlerhafte Genehmigungen im Umweltrecht', in *Festschrift für Kurt Repmann zum 65. Geburtstag*, München, 1989, 241–257 and Rudolphi, H.J., 'Strafrechtliche Verantwortlichkeit der Bediensteten von Betrieben für Gewässerverunreihnigungen und Begrenzung durch den Einleitungsbescheid', in *Festschrift für Karl Lackner zum 70. Geburtstag am 18. Februar 1987*, Berlin, 1987, 837–887.

38 See Roef, D., *Strafbare overheden. Een rechtsvergelijkende studie naar de strafrechtelijke aanprakelijkheid van overheden voor milieuverstoring*, Antwerp, Intersentia, 2001, 531–544.

plant.[39] However, the majority of these provisions are limited to private persons; only the provisions of water pollution and waste disposal are applicable to both private persons and civil servants. This is disputed in relation to soil pollution. In 1994, the last reform of environmental crimes took place.[40] However, the German legislator saw no reasonable grounds for extending the responsibility of civil servants. Yet, it makes no sense to place under criminal pressure only those civil servants who are engaged in protecting water and controlling waste. If there is a need for criminal sanctions imposed on civil servants, then there can be no reasonable ground for dismissing principally those civil servants engaged in controlling the protection of air, which means special rules for environmental offences by public servants with a general application to all pollution should be introduced. Therefore, the solution of the Spanish legislator could in principle be recommended. However, incorporating as the Spanish legislator did provisions into a special part of the criminal code, thereby amending the basic principles set in the general part of the criminal code, is an ongoing problem. Nevertheless, excessive criminalization is not a concern in Spain because negligent behaviour is excluded from criminal law.

7.2 Addressees

In most of the Member States, criminal or administrative penal liability in the context of fulfilling administrative tasks is limited to natural persons. However, in the United Kingdom, only the government departments as such are immune (crown immunity), local authorities (and the Environment Agency) can be held criminally liable. The criminal liability of administrative agencies as such is a completely new question for most of the continental European countries. However, the criminal liability of municipalities has a long tradition in Denmark, and in Germany non-criminal fines can be

---

[39] For an introduction to environmental criminal law in Germany and the texts of the provisions of the criminal code see Faure, M. and Heine, G., *Environmental criminal law in the European Union*, 143–164.

[40] See Heine, G., 'Umweltstrafrecht im Rechtsstaat', *Zeitschrift für Umweltrecht*, 1995, 63–71; Breuer, R., 'Verwaltungsrechtlicher und strafrechtlicher Umweltschutz – vom ersten zum zweiten Umweltkriminalitätsgesetz', *Juristenzeitung*, 1994, 1077–1091; Kloepfer, M. and Vierhaus, H.P., *Umweltstrafrecht*, München, 1995; Möhrenschlager, M., 'Revision des Umweltstrafrechts. Das zweite Gesetz zur Bekämpfung der Umweltkriminalität', *Neue Zeitschrift für Strafrecht*, 1994, 513–519 and 566–569; Schmidt, A. and Schöne, Th., 'Das neue Umweltstrafrecht', *Neue Juristische Wochenschrift*, 1994, 2514–2519.

imposed.[41] Furthermore, all the countries which have recently adopted criminal liability of legal persons or are under discussion in this field (see above, § 1) will be under political pressure to deal with the criminal liability of administrative agencies as such. By opening the door to criminal law being imposed on legal persons, the natural consequence is discussion on integrating administrative agencies into the criminal liability regime.

In most countries, the national legislators give environmental agencies wide discretion to apply their powers to protect the environment. As a rule, wide discretion and social responsibility should correspond (in certain cases) to legal liability, -taking into consideration the assertion underlining criminal liability of enterprises. However, prosecuting administrative agencies or government departments is alien to many legal systems. The strongest arguments against this approach is the principle of immunity and the sharing of power. Indeed, this possible constraint on the executive by the judiciary is an ongoing and unresolved issue. However, a detailed discussion would focus on the objectives of a criminal law and on whether new adequate sanctions should be taken into consideration. For example, in Canada the government of the Northwest Territories was sentenced by a criminal court to a rather symbolic sanction in the case of environmental pollution (failing to prevent sewage discharge).

7.3 Importance of the criminal provisions – effects

Provisions criminalizing the illegal behaviour of civil servants which causes pollution seems not to play an important role in the legal systems of the Member States, considering the number of sentences. The number of convictions of civil servants for environmental pollution remains indeed rather low. However, even a few convictions may have a significant impact in general terms. Consider, for example, the situation in Germany: it is obvious that the two leading cases of the German federal Supreme Court had echoed through the administrative bodies. Furthermore, a high number of preliminary investigations indicates a change in the culture of enforcement. Indeed, in many countries it is obvious that the threat presented by criminal law influences administrative behaviour.

The other side of the coin is, however, that administrative agencies are usually given broad discretion in implementing environmental policy. It seems to be a structural consequence, because the national legislators increasingly give power to the executive bodies. Because in most countries strict

41 The so-called 'Bußgelder' in case of 'Ordnungswidrigkeiten'.

organizational and procedural distinctions between criminal law on the one hand and administrative law on the other do exist, there should be no question that the exercise of this administrative discretion should be taboo for the prosecutors. Therefore, only clear cases of illegal behaviour, such as granting illegal permission or collaborating with an enterprise and causing pollution should lead to criminal liability. Therefore, it can be recommended to follow in principle the legal route taken by the Netherlands, Germany and Spain.

8. MISCELLANEOUS

8.1 Effectiveness of administrative sanctions as a deterrent

The first question put in the section entitled miscellaneous is whether the administrative sanctions (some of which were discussed above in sections 4 and 5) are as effective a deterrent as criminal penalties (discussed in 3). The respondents answered this question based on experience in their countries. It is interesting that the approach chosen in the questionnaire itself is to examine the effectiveness of administrative sanctions as a *deterrent*. This deterrence perspective was also chosen in analyzing the effectiveness of criminal penalties (see question 3), although it is recognized that other approaches could be applied as well. In line with the discussion on criminal penalties and with legal doctrine, most respondents argue that from a strict deterrence perspective monetary administrative sanctions are in principle as effective as criminal sanctions. With respect to Germany, it is, for instance, mentioned that administrative fines with a maximum of 1 m. DM (usually 100,000 DM, in practice they are approximate) can be imposed. Also, with respect to Italy, it is mentioned that administrative sanctions are in principle even more effective since they can affect offenders' wealth directly. Indeed, other things being equal, one could argue that if only monetary sanctions were to be imposed, administrative sanctions could in principle be as effective as criminal sanctions and possibly swifter and at lower cost, since usually the procedural requirements for administrative legal procedures are lower than in criminal procedures.

This result might, however, change when non-monetary sanctions are considered. It was argued above that as soon as the expected fine exceeds the offenders' wealth and hence an insolvency problem arises, monetary sanctions might become ineffective, given the underdeterrence problems.[42] This problem might arise relatively quickly, since to be an effective deterrent

---

[42] See Shavell, S., 'Criminal law and the optimal use of non-monetary sanctions as a deterrent', *Columbia Law Review*, 1985, vol. 85, 1232–1262.

expected fines should be relatively high to outweigh any potential benefits to the offender given the low detection rate. However, non-monetary sanctions should of course not necessarily be limited to the traditional prison sanction. In cases of corporate environmental crime in particular, one could think of a wide variety of administrative penalties which could be very effective as well and which might well be imposed through an effective administrative procedure. The aim is to provide the Member State with an effective 'toolkit'.

At first sight, there are therefore various advantages to applying administrative sanctions, and these are also stressed by the respondents. There are, however, also several drawbacks, having to do with both fairness and effectiveness. An aspect of fairness that one should bear in mind is that some administrative sanctions could be considered equally severe by the offender. This could be true for very high administrative fines, but especially for very far-reaching administrative measures, such as the shutdown of a specific installation. In its legal doctrine and case law, the European Court of Human Rights has held that under certain circumstances those administrative sanctions should also be considered penalties to which the guarantees of Article 6 of the European Convention on Human Rights should be applied. This means that the administrative procedures of the various Member States, by which these administrative sanctions are imposed, should then at least meet the minimum requirements of Article 6 ECHR. This means that many of the apparent advantages of, for instance, reduced time and effectiveness of an administrative procedure might not be that great compared to the criminal procedure. In addition, one should bear in mind that the criminal procedure also has a number of other guarantees, aiming at guaranteeing the defendant a fair trial, which means that the rule of law character of the criminal process often still is substantially higher when compared with an administrative procedure. This could be an argument in favour of the criminal procedure, especially in cases where sanctions with far-reaching consequences (imprisonment) could be imposed. In this respect, it should also be mentioned that in order to apply criminal law, various principles of criminal law must be respected as well, which can be seen as a guarantee for both the offender and the quality of the criminal procedure. Obviously, this may have drawbacks as far as effectiveness is concerned. It is therefore understandable that the German respondent expresses enthusiasm about the administrative fine procedure in relation to the liability of corporations, since it also allows for high fines to be imposed against companies, fines that – until now – would have been impossible under traditional German criminal law, given the principle of guilt.

Some law and economics scholars have also articulated a powerful argument in favour of administrative sanctions based on error costs. They argue that one reason to have the large protection provided by the criminal procedure (high evidentiary standards, presumption of innocence, etc.) is that the consequences of the criminal law for citizens can be quite harsh. Hence, the criminal procedure should have a high guarantee that innocent people are not convicted. The costs of punishing the innocent (in economic terms referred to as 'error costs') are of course quite high if, for example, imprisonment is wrongfully imposed. This justifies applying the costly criminal procedure when potentially harsh sanctions can be applied. However, the same argument does not apply when only monetary sanctions, such as fines, are at stake. In that case, the error costs are substantially lower and there is no objection to using the cheaper administrative procedure. Therefore, from an economic perspective, it does make sense to use administrative sanctions (provided of course that they remain relatively modest) and an administrative procedure in case of minor offences and to reserve the more costly criminal procedure and criminal sanctions for the more serious infringements.

It is obviously not possible to make a final analysis of the trade-off between administrative sanctions and criminal penalties within the scope of this report. One should only bear in mind that it might at first seem attractive to rely more on the apparent effectiveness of administrative sanctions, but that this might come at a cost as far as the elements of fair trial and the rule of law character of the procedure is concerned. Once the price for increased effectiveness is considered too high, this might be an argument in favour of using the criminal law supported by full guarantees.

Such an argument could also be made on effectiveness grounds. Some respondents have difficulties with the fact that administrative law enforcement is, a point that is also mentioned in the literature, inevitably based on a negotiation process between the enforcing administrative bodies on the one hand and the offender on the other.[43] Some, for instance the Dutch respondent, argue that this attitude of negotiations is negative, since the administrative authorities would spend too much time negotiating with the offenders, would have a naive belief in the trustworthiness of the offenders and wait too long before imposing sanctions. This view of administrative law enforcement corresponds with the finding in the literature on public choice where it has indeed been stressed that a risk inherent to administrative law enforcement is that administrative agencies might be 'captured' by the industry which they must regulate and control. This risk of capture is especially great in areas such

---

[43] See Diez, J. and Gniting, J., 'Koordinationsprobleme zwischen Verwaltungs- und Strafrechtsimplementation im Umweltbereich', *Monatschrift für Kriminologie und Strafrechtreform*, 1989, 190–211 and Aalders, M.V.C., 'De politiefunctie van de bijzondere opsporingsambtenaar', *Tijdschrift voor Criminologie*, 1980, 287–298.

as environmental risk, where the technological information is available in particular to the regulated and less so to the offenders. Others, however, stress that this approach to negotiation taken by the administrative authorities need not necessarily be judged as counterproductive. As long as there is no true capture, whereby the administrative authorities merely serve the interests of industry, negotiations leading to compliance with legislation might be far more effective than lengthy trials with the imposition of an ineffective sanction.[44] It is, again, not possible within the scope of this report, to judge which of the two approaches would be the more effective.

It is anyway correct that a key difference between administrative and criminal law enforcement is that within administrative law enforcement there will be a closer connection between the regulated industry and the enforcer than there would be with criminal law enforcement. This is simply a result of the fact that administrative law enforcement has a stronger basis in negotiating with a view to compliance than in sanctioning with a view to deterring. The latter is still the traditional goal of criminal law enforcement. This lack of distance of administrative law enforcement is of course criticized in, for instance, the Italian and Dutch reports.

Perhaps the two approaches can be reconciled by considering the *ultimum remedium* approach towards criminal law enforcement, as proposed in the German report. There is trust that usually the administrative bodies first try to achieve compliance by using effective administrative tools (such as administrative orders and prohibitions). Only if these fail, would criminal prosecution apply. Many offenders have sought an administrative 'regularization' by the time they must appear in court. If this is the case, either there will be no prosecution at all or only a fine will be imposed. A drawback to such an *ultimum remedium* approach is that it of course substantially reduces the role of the criminal law in protecting ecological values. In addition, in all cases where administrative enforcement would lead to the imposition of a modest administrative fine, there is still no guarantee of effective compliance. This might be especially problematic in cases where administrative fines are indeed too low because the procedure has been influenced by collusion between the authorities and the industry. In addition, it could be argued that, no matter what happens at the administrative level, some violations of ecological values are important enough for criminal law to intervene directly. That argument of course relies on the assumption that there is an important and

---

44 See on the role of administrative agencies also Ogus, A. and Abbot, C., 'Pollution and penalties', in Swanson, T. (ed.), An introduction to the law and economics of environmental policy: issues in institutional design, JAI Press, 2002, 493–516.

direct role for criminal law in protecting ecological values[45] (if these are seriously endangered), also in cases where in principle administrative fines or other sanctions could be applied. Obviously, the central question is not so much whether a legal system should choose between administrative or criminal law protection of the environment, but more how to strike the right balance between the two systems. Some support for such an independent and direct role for the criminal law can be drawn for instance from the Council of Europe Convention on the Protection of the Environment through Criminal Law. Article 6 indeed provides that in case of serious endangerment of environmental values (as provided in Arts. 2 and 3) parties must take appropriate measures to make those offences punishable by criminal sanctions which take into account the serious nature of these offences.

In sum, it is, as the Finnish country report mentions, difficult to compare administrative sanctions and criminal penalties at a very abstract level. Both can be effective in specific situations. One should, however, bear in mind that within this effectiveness one should also take into account the impartiality problems that may always occur in case of administrative law enforcement and balance them against the benefits of an effective negotiation process that leads to compliance. In addition, rule of law aspects such as the quality of the administrative versus the criminal legal procedure and the fair trial principle should be taken into account when the choice between administrative and criminal law enforcement is made. Obviously, the outcome of this debate will very much depend upon the gravity and seriousness of the facts.

8.2 Tolerance in case of 'technical breaches'

A second important question under the 'miscellaneous' section concerns the question of whether in principle an administrative sanction or a criminal penalty is always imposed for most breaches of environmental law or whether there is a tolerance for minor breaches. The example given is one of technical breaches of a permit (for instance, violations of an administrative condition to report) without environmental harm as a consequence.

This is an exceedingly interesting but difficult topic, which is of importance

---

45 It has been stressed in German legal doctrine in particular that criminal law should aim at the protection of legal interests and values (Rechtsgüterschutz) and that therefore environmental criminal law should aim at the protection of ecological interests. See e.g. Heine, G., 'Zur historischen Entwicklung normativen Umweltschutzes', *Goltdammer's Archiv für Strafrecht*, 1989, vol. 136, 116–131 and Heine, G., 'Allemagne. Crimes against the environment', *International Review of Penal Law*, 1994, 731–759.

not only for environmental law. It relates to the general question in administrative and criminal law of whether the administrative and criminal law enforcers should in principle attempt to prosecute every possible violation or whether taking into account policy evaluations in the decision is permitted. It is well known that the legal systems in Western Europe differ in that respect.[46] Some, for instance Belgium and the Netherlands, apply the so-called 'principle of discretion', which means that the public prosecutor should in a specific case assess whether it is expedient to bring a criminal prosecution or not. However, in these legal systems usually the 'prosecution policy' of the public ministry is also regulated in some manner. For instance in Belgium, a circular from the attorneys general provides that the reasons for a dismissal must be provided. Dismissals can also take place for expedient reasons such as the nature of the facts (little social repercussion of the facts) or the personality of the offender. The general tenor of that circular is, however, that serious offences may not be dismissed for expedient reasons. Other countries, for instance Germany, have a different approach. In that country, the public prosecutor should in principle prosecute every case.[47] However, also in Germany a number of significant exceptions exist, so that the differences may not be that great in practice.

Taking these issues into consideration, specifically in the environmental context, the question of whether one should prosecute every case will to a great extent depend upon the goal one has with an administrative or criminal prosecution. If strict deterrence is the goal, then there is strong support for the formal position that as soon as the law has been breached, the intention of the legislator should be followed and every case should be prosecuted. An argument against that is precisely an effectiveness point that the capacity of the criminal system in every country respecting the rule of law is limited. Hence, within every system, choices will have to be made which could lead to the reasoning that specific minor cases should not be prosecuted but dealt with otherwise.

However, in environmental law one should take care when qualifying a

---

46 For an overview of prosecution policy in the EU Member States see the contributions in Van den Wyngaert, Ch. (ed.), *Criminal procedure systems in the European Community*, London, Butterworths, 1993.

47 See on the non-prosecution policies in Germany e.g. Richter, Th. and Dernauer, M., 'Historical development of non-prosecution policies in Germany', in Albrecht, H.-J. and Guang Zhong, Ch. (eds.), *Non-prosecution policies. A sino-German comparision*, Max Planck Institute for foreign and international criminal law, Freiburg im Breisgau, 2002, 19–40 and Kilchling, M., 'Non-prosecution policies and (judicial) control in Germany', in Albrecht, H.-J. and Guang Zhong, Ch. (eds.), *Non-prosecution policies. A sino-German comparision*, Max Planck Institute for foreign and international criminal law, Freiburg im Breisgau, 2002, 173–184.

violation of a regulatory standard or a permit condition necessarily as a mere 'technical breach'. In some cases, where it constitutes merely a duty to report, this might indeed be the case. But even under such circumstances, one could argue that such a duty to report enables enforcing bodies to perform their enforcement duties. In other cases, a violation of a permit condition might actually lead to environmental harm. The latter can of course be the case if emission standards are violated. It will certainly be less likely that it will be tolerated when violation actually leads to environmental harm. Nevertheless, there might be an effectiveness argument against prosecution. This is particularly true if one wishes to see the role of the public prosecutor as one of negotiating with the offender, compelling him or her to restore harm done. In some countries, for instance in Belgium and the Netherlands, such negotiations, leading to repairing harm done, is considered far more effective than actual prosecution.

In sum, no matter how it is formulated on paper, every legal system will somehow accept tolerance for minor breaches, especially in cases where ecological values are not endangered. On paper, there are still differences. Denmark, Austria and Portugal report that tolerance is not accepted and also that formal breaches that result in no harm should in any event be prosecuted and fined. Finland and the Netherlands seem to accept tolerance for minor breaches as a matter of policy. In Germany, minor criminal offences may be discontinued if certain conditions are fulfilled (such as restitution, order to bring the functioning of an installation in line with ecological standards by additional investments). Furthermore, the United Kingdom reports that minor incidents with no negative effect on the environment can be settled with a warning. Italy reports that there is often tolerance, but as the (tragic) consequence of collusion with the public authorities. It is remarkable that the legal systems that report that no tolerance is accepted, they all state that the sanction imposed will in any event be in line with the degree of the breach and with the damage caused (Denmark, Germany, Spain). Thus the fact that the breach was only a formal one, which did not harm the environment, will be taken into account when determining the level of the sanction.

The result may therefore be that in some countries minor breaches will effectively lead to a mere warning or to the absence of any formal reaction. In other countries, there will be a fine (or even a prosecution), but the absence of environmental harm will nevertheless be taken into account in the level of the sanction.

An important final question is which authority has the right to decide on the influence of tolerance. This once more relates to the relationship between administrative and criminal law enforcement and to whether the criminal sanction (and procedure) should only be used as an *ultimum remedium*. In

Germany, administrative bodies apparently often first try to use effective administrative tools and the public prosecution in industrial cases acts mostly when administrative law enforcement has failed. In the Netherlands, less reliance appears to be placed on administrative bodies. The public prosecution believes they make too much effort to reach agreements with industry. For that reason, the government wants to limit the tolerance by administrative bodies and prefers to leave the decision regarding whether or not to prosecute minor breaches as a policy matter with the public prosecutor. The latter is true in Belgium as well.

8.3 Information and the role of intelligence services

The final question is related to the role of intelligence services in the enforcement of environmental law. Some countries, such as Austria, Italy, the Netherlands, Portugal, Spain and the United Kingdom, report that some form of intelligence services do indeed play a role in environmental cases, although according to the United Kingdom report this would only be the case in major waste transfer cases.[48] Others, such as Denmark, Finland and Germany, report that intelligence services would not play any specific role in environmental cases. The same is true for Belgium, although it was reported that in the few cases in which intelligence services did play a role, it was on the basis of information provided by a foreign 'intelligence service' (usually from the Netherlands).

The question of information in the enforcement of environmental law is of course a very important one and for various reasons. Data on the prior history of specific offenders, prior cases, and so on, might on the one hand be very important, during the licensing process and during the preliminary investigation, but on the other hand it is always possible that this constitutes an significant infringement of the privacy of the persons involved. One should also bear in mind that in some cases information is of course gathered, but not through a formal involvement of intelligence services. In some cases, enforcing bodies themselves or specialized prosecution officers might keep records of, for instance, criminal networks that are active in the illegal transfer of waste.

The respondents report that in cases where the information of intelligence services is apparently used, the co-operation between those services, the

---

48 See Lavrysen, L., 'Judicial responses in the nineties to Dutch (and German) shipments of waste to Belgium in the eighties', *Maastricht Journal of European and Comparative Law*, 1995, 219–234.

police and enforcement bodies did not give rise to specific problems. The Italian report mentions that in some cases the police receive input from intelligence services which may lead to opening a preliminary investigation. This might not be possible under all legal systems, since the question could be asked during the trial whether it was possible to check the information provided through the intelligence service. This is of course a difficult topic when so-called anonymous witnesses have been used. These issues, for instance, whether classified information received from intelligence services may be used to begin a preliminary investigation, of course do not have a strong connection to national legal procedure. The Netherlands reports good co-operation between the intelligence services and the police, which would not pose specific problems since there is less secret information provided by the intelligence services. Otherwise, the problem regarding guaranteeing anonymity of the source, which is mentioned in the United Kingdom report, could arise.

All country reports mention that the information supplied through the intelligence services can be used afterwards in court. Presumably, this means that the information has been provided in accordance with the specific national rules, which then obviously must be followed up.

CONCLUDING REMARKS

A first important result is indeed that the current exercise has allowed insight to be gained into the criminal enforcement of environmental law in legal practice. There has thus been some added value compared to the previous report (environmental criminal law in the European Union),[1] which mainly addressed substantive environmental criminal law as laid down in legislation. This insight into the legal practice of criminal enforcement of environmental law in various countries is of course useful, since it may encourage the trans-boundary co-operation between the various authorities by providing a better understanding of the various policies pursued. Thus, this insight can also contribute to a better implementation of European environmental law.

1. TREND: TOWARDS CORPORATE CRIMINAL LIABILITY

If one must identify certain trends in legislation or case law with respect to environmental criminal law in the countries that were examined, one might point to the clear trend towards some form of corporate criminal liability. This currently seems to be one of the most debated issues in environmental legal policy with respect to the use of criminal law. Increasingly, one is aware of the fact that serious environmental crimines are often (but not always) corporate crimes, which can therefore almost not be handled by traditional criminal law, which almost inevitably focuses on the natural person. One can

1 See Faure, M. and Heine, G., Environmental criminal law in the European Union, 2000.

therefore see increasing discussions, at least at the policy level, towards the introduction of corporate criminal liability in the legal systems where this does not already exist. Most legal systems already do provide for sanctions that can be applied specifically to legal entities. It mostly consists of either (administrative) penal sanctions or confiscation. Usually, it is argued that these sanctions do not have a criminal character and can therefore be imposed in some but not all relevant countries, even if an individual's guilt has not been proved. However, looking at legal practice, one notices that the so-called Verbandsgeldbuße in Germany or confiscation in other countries do not play a key role. Hence, introducing criminal corporate liability that functions properly should be discussed. However, one should be aware of the fact that introducing such liability alone will of course not solve all problems. This can be seen in the legal systems which already have a form of corporate criminal liability. These systems often cope with problems in case law, since they often lack clear criteria to impute illegal acts of individuals to the corporation. Hence, the introduction of corporate criminal liability should be combined with clear criteria of imputability and sanctions.

Of course, the fact that serious environmental crimes are often corporate crimes should also be taken into account with respect to other aspects of the criminal enforcement system as well. This increasing interest in corporate liability has for instance also caused an increasing interest in the criminal liability of public legal entities and public servants when they have contributed to environmental pollution. Although there are not many cases in that respect yet, one can undoubtedly detect a tendency towards increasing the responsibility of public servants working with environmental agencies.

The corporate character of environmental crime should also be taken into account at the level of sanctioning. So far, legal systems often only use the administrative penal system for corporate crime. This calls for general questions concerning the role of these administrative penal sanctions in addition to the criminal penalties. It is now generally held that these administrative penal sanctions can be quite useful, especially when they consist of direct measures aiming at repairing environmental harm. However, one should be aware of the fact that an administrative procedure cannot provide the same guarantees as the criminal trial; therefore one should bear in mind that not all enforcement of environmental law can be entrusted to these administrative penal systems. Moreover, it should always be examined whether these administrative penal sanctions in fact have a goal that differs from that of the criminal penalty. Were this not the case, then a double reaction would be provided against one similar offence, which might conflict with the *ne bis in idem* principle.

As far as criminal penalties are concerned, a relatively rare use of sanctions other than fines was observed. This is not only true as far as the prison sanction is concerned (which is reserved for only the most serious cases), but also for the so-called prohibition orders. These orders, aimed at the prohibition of carrying out a certain activity or profession (which can be either administrative or criminal in character), are almost never imposed in practice. When corporate criminal liability is introduced, increasing use should be made of sanctions which can be directed towards the legal entity itself. Indeed, legal systems should be aware of the fact that other sanctions might be more appropriate for legal entities than for natural persons. It is striking that even in legal systems which do have corporate criminal liability, such as the Netherlands, corporate sanctions are almost never used. Instead, one can observe a kind of negotiation process between administrative agencies and the offender will take place, whereby administrative agencies seek the offender's compliance with environmental law. Through these kind of informal mechanisms, often the same result is reached, which should in principle be achieved by corporate sanctions. This then obviously also explains why these are not often used in practice.

2. ADMINISTRATIVE OR CRIMINAL LAW?

These informal negotiation procedures are the subject of a great deal of debate. Proponents stress the effectiveness of negotiations by administrative agencies which can result in compliance or in administrative penal sanctions. This model of co-operation between administrative agencies and offenders, however, raises questions with respect to their ability to investigate effectively when negotiations do not lead to the desired result. Another criticism is that often those negotiations take place without effective control by the public prosecutor. Therefore, some have argued that the administrative agencies should have a duty to report every crime to the public prosecutor; in that case, the final decision on whether to prosecute would still be in the hands of the prosecutor. This issue is obviously very much connected to the role of the investigating authorities and public prosecutors within the national criminal procedure. Some countries where the public prosecutor is in principle forced to prosecute every crime (the so-called principle of mandatory prosecution), for instance Austria, will of course have difficulty accepting negotiations by administrative authorities, and this could result in environmental crimes not being reported and prosecuted. However, in countries where it is accepted that the public prosecutor should not prosecute every crime (e.g., the Netherlands), criticism is also heard with respect to administrative agencies keeping environmental cases 'to themselves' in a negotiation process for too long, whereby it would take too long before formal criminal proceedings would take place.

However, it is certainly not only the administrative authorities that negotiate with offenders. This may be true for the public prosecutor as well. Some cases are simply not prosecuted because they constitute minor offences (*de minimis non curat praetor*); in other cases, the prosecutor tries to achieve compliance by cautioning the offender that he or she can be prosecuted if certain conditions are not met. These informal mechanisms are to some extent the result of very broad criminal provisions which give a great deal of power to the public prosecutor via the negotiation processes. These negotiations might ultimately be successful, because a corporation will, for instance, often prefer to comply with the public prosecutor's conditions if it, by doing so, can avoid prosecution with a public hearing and the resulting bad publicity. Nevertheless, one can raise serious questions whether the systematic use of these kinds of negotiation processes (which is apparently the case in environmental criminal law enforcement in some legal systems) is acceptable from the perspective of democracy and the rule of law. One can indeed question whether the prosecutor has sufficiently examined the conditions of criminal liability and whether the rights of the defence are fully respected during these negotiation processes, which sometimes take place under the threat of 'going to the press'. Also, one could question whether it should be the task of the public prosecutor to in fact impose sanctions or if this should only take place after an impartial judge has established, during a public hearing, that the conditions for criminal liability are met. However, summary convictions and various reductions of hearings (for instance Strafbefehle in Germany) which play a role in environmental cases do relax these approaches but are of great practical importance. This shift from the decisive powers with respect to the limits of criminal liability from the judge to the public prosecutor and the administrative agencies is certainly open to criticism. Indeed, one of the effects is obviously that it is no longer an impartial judge who decides whether all the conditions for criminal liability are actually fulfilled. The risk exists that, because of the threat of criminal prosecution, the person against whom only a suspicion of an environmental offence exists will be tempted to agree to pay a high fine or perform certain acts in order to avoid prosecution. Moreover, the publicity of the oral hearing may also have an additional deterrent effect and therefore even be desirable from a policy perspective. Nonetheless, not every case should go to a public hearing, given the expense involved. Therefore, one can certainly expect to see a trend in the legislation of the European Member States towards an increased use in the future of (administrative) systems to deal with smaller (environmental) offences.

3. TOWARDS A EUROPEAN ENVIRONMENTAL CRIMINAL LAW?

Obviously, this study shows that to some extent there are similarities (for instance, the central role of the public prosecutor in criminal law enforcement and the combined use of administrative and criminal sanctions), but that there are also important differences between the practices in the European Member States. Differences sometimes relate to substantive criminal law (for instance with respect to the criminal liability of enterprises or with respect to the rights of victims to initiate criminal prosecution), but in other cases there were mainly differences between the environmental awareness in the Member States. It is for instance striking to note that the Italian report mentions that environmental awareness in that country is still low, compared to for instance Nordic countries such as Denmark where environmental consciousness is very high. This variance in environmental awareness of course influences the effectiveness of criminal enforcement of environmental law as well. If environmental awareness is low, individuals might for instance not be very willing to report violations of environmental legislation to the police.

The fact that one can easily point to differences between legal practices in Member States inevitably raises the question whether there is a need for further harmonization. It is relatively easy to make a – politically correct – argument that, given remaining differences between Member States, one should strive for further harmonization. However, one should take into account that in this report only legal practices were addressed, not differences in substantive environmental criminal law.[2] It is obviously much easier to harmonize substantive environmental law than legal practice.

In addition, one should note that increased co-operation and co-ordination between Member States, as regards the criminal enforcement of environmental law, is possible, even with remaining differences. One important starting point for such an increased collaboration is a good knowledge of the other legal systems. This report provides a modest attempt at improving the knowledge. Moreover, various efforts to harmonize environmental criminal law as

---

2 These differences are, in a broader environmental legal perspective addressed for instance by Seerden, R., Heldeweg, M. and Deketelaere, K. (eds.), *Public environmental law in the European Union and the United States. A comparative analysis*, The Hague, Kluwer Law International, 2002 and by Koeman, N.S.J. (ed.), *Environmental law in Europe*, The Hague, Kluwer Law International, 1999. These differences were addressed inter alia in Faure, M. and Heine, G., *Environmental Criminal Law in the European Union*, as well as in Faure, M. and Heine, G., <http://www.europa.eu.int/comm/environment/crime/criminal_penalties.pdf>

well were considered. Reference can again be made to the Convention on the Protection of the Environment through Criminal Law of the Council of Europe and to the resolutions of the XVth International Congress of Penal Law of the AIDP. Hence, it might be better to await the results of these initiatives before starting any new ones, for instance, attempting to harmonize legal practices. One should also bear in mind that harmonizing legal practices as far as criminal law enforcement is concerned might be a very difficult, if not impossible, task. Indeed, many of the differences discussed in this report do not relate much to differences in environmental law, but rather to differences in substantive criminal law. These issues, such as the role of the victim in the criminal process, might be related to the cultural identity of the specific Member State in such a way that it does not seem realistic that these differences would be changed (if necessary at all), just for the sake of improving the enforcement of environmental law.

There are, moreover, a few other recent developments in the area of environmental criminal law in Europe that are certainly worth mentioning. The European Commission adopted a Proposal for a Directive of the European Parliament and of the Council on the Protection of the Environment through Criminal Law on 13 March 2001.[3] This Proposal for a Directive was based on the first error and required Member States impose criminal penalties for breaches of the Community Directives and Regulations listed in its annex. The proposal hence forced Member States to introduce criminal laws related to the violation of specific environmental directives. This was considered a necessary cure for the lack of enforcement. The proposal led to fierce criticism from many criminal lawyers in the Member States.[4] The criticism holds that it would be better to use administrative sanctions to enforce environmental law, at least several scholars argue that a mere focus on criminal law is too one-sided.

Meanwhile the Council of the European Union adopted a Framework Decision on the Protection of the Environment through Criminal Law. It was based on a Danish initiative taken in February 2000 with a view to adopting a Council Framework Decision on combating serious environmental crime. This Framework Decision originally only obliged Member States to introduce criminal sanctions for offences considered 'serious environmental crimes'. However, in a later version, which received final acceptance and was adopted on 27 January 2003, the Council adopted a Framework Decision which was very much inspired by the Council of Europe Convention.

3 COM (2001) 139 final – *OJ* C-180/238 of 26 June 2001.

4 See for instance in the Netherlands Buruma, Y. and Somsen, J., 'Een strafwetgever te Brussel inzake milieubescherming?', *Nederlands Juristenblad*, 2001, 795–797.

Clearly, the fact that two parallel texts existed concerning the protection of the environment through criminal law was considered a significant problem, indicating the difficulties in defining the exact competences between the so-called 'first pillar' (on which the Proposal for a Directive is based) and the so-called 'third pillar' on which the Framework decision is based. Consequently, the Commission launched a complaint against the Framework Decision of 27 January 2003 to the European Court of Justice, arguing that the Council was not competent in the area of environmental criminal law.[5]

It is, at this stage, not certain how the European Court of Justice will decide the matter. It is, nevertheless, equally clear that the approaches chosen by the European Commission on the one hand and the European Council on the other are fundamentally different. On the one hand, the Commission apparently deems it necessary to introduce criminal law as a remedy for the lack of enforcement. The obligation to impose criminal sanctions is thus limited to specific cases of breaches of legislation implementing European environmental law. The Council's Framework Decision on the other hand follows more the approach in the Convention on the Protection of the Environment through Criminal Law and seeks a more general harmonization of environmental criminal law, providing a minimum standard of environmental offences.

---

5 For an overview of the arguments see Comte, F., 'Criminal environmental law and Community competence', *European Environmental Law Review*, 2003, 147–156.

LIST OF REFERENCES

Albrecht, H.J. and Leppä, S. (eds.), *Criminal Law and the Environment*, Helsinki, HEUNI, 1992.

Bocken, H. and Ryckbost, D. (eds.), Codification of Environmental Law, Proceedings of an International Conference, The Hague, Kluwer, 1996.

De Witte, B., 'Sovereignty and European Integration: the Weight of Legal Traditions', *Maastricht Journal of European and Comparative Law*, 1995, 145–174.

Eser, A. and Heine, G. (eds.), *Umweltstrafrecht in England, Kanada und den USA*, Max-Planck-Institut für ausländisches und internationales Strafrecht, Freiburg im Breisgau, 1994.

Faure, M. and Oudijk, J., 'Die strafgerichtliche Überprüfung von Verwaltungsakten im Umweltrecht', *Juristen Zeitung*, 1994, 86–91.

Faure, M., 'Ius Commune and Transboundary Environmental Pollution', *Maastricht Journal of European and Comparative Law*, 1995, 215–218.

Faure, M. and Lefevere, J., 'Introduction to European Environmental Law', in Aspen, P. et al, *Shipping Law Faces Europe: European Policy, Competition and Environment*, Antwerp, Maklu, 1995, 93–107.

Faure, M. and Visser, M., 'How to Punish Environmental Pollution? Some Reflections on Various Models of Criminalization of Environmental Harm', *European Journal of Crime, Criminal Law and Criminal Justice*, 1995, 316–368.

Faure, M., 'Criminal Penalties', in Bocken, H. and Ryckbost, D. (eds.), *Codification of Environmental Law. Draft Decree on Environmental Policy*, The Hague, Kluwer, 1996, 202–207.

Faure, M., 'Het Nederlands milieustrafrecht: dringend aan herziening toe!', *Rechtsgeleerd Magazijn Themis*, 1997, 3–12.

Greer, D. (ed.), *Compensating Crime Victims, a European Survey*, Freiburg im Breisgau, Max Planck Institut für ausländisches und internationales Strafrecht, 1996.

Heine, G., 'Aspekte des Umweltstrafrechts im internationalen Vergleich', *Golt-dammer's Archiv für Strafrecht*, 1986, 67–88.

Heine, G., 'Environmental Criminality and its Control', in Eser, A. and Thormundsson, J. (eds.), *Old Ways and New Needs in Criminal Legislation*, Freiburg im Breisgau, Max Planck Institute for Comparative and International Law, 1989, 255–279.

Heine, G., 'Verwaltungsakzessorietät des Umweltstrafrechts', *Neue juristische Wochenschrift*, 1990, 2425–2434.

Heine, G., 'International Conference on Environmental Criminal Law', *Zeitschrift für die gesamte Strafrechtswissenschaft*, 1991, 819–827.

Heine, G., Die strafrechtliche Verantwortlichkeit von Unternehmen, von individuellen Fehlverhalten zu kollektiven Fehlentwicklungen insbesondere bei Großrisiken, Baden-Baden, Nomos, 1995.

Heine, G., 'Criminal Liability of Enterprises and New Risks. International Developments – National Consequences', *Maastricht Journal of European and Comparative Law*, 1995, 107–128.

Heine, G., 'Von individueller zu kollektiver Verantwortlichkeit. Einige Grundfragen der aktuellen Kriminalpolitik', in Arnold, J., Burkhardt, B., Gropp, W. and Koch, H.-G. (eds.), *Grenzüberschreitungen, Beiträge zum 60. Geburtstag von Albin Eser*, Freiburg im Breisgau, Max Planck Institut für ausländisches und internationales Strafrecht, 1995, 51–78.

Heine, G., 'Die strafrechtliche Verantwortlichkeit von Unternehmen: internationale Entwicklung – nationale Konsequenzen', *Österreichische Juristen Zeitung*, 1996, 211–219.

Heine, G., Prabhu, M. and Alvazzi del Frate, A. (eds.), *Environmental Protection – Potentials and Limits of Criminal Justice*, Max-Planck-Institut für ausländisches und internationales Strafrecht, Freiburg im Breisgau, 1997.

Heine, G. (ed.), *Umweltstrafrecht in mittel- und südeuropäischen Ländern*, Max-Planck-Institut für ausländisches und internationales Strafrecht, Freiburg im Breisgau, 1997.

Jans, J., *European Environmental Law*, Kluwer Law International, 1995.

Kötz, H., 'A Common Private Law for Europe: Perspectives for the Reform of European Legal Education', in De Witte, B. and Forder, C. (eds.), *The Common Law of Europe and the Future of Legal Education*, Deventer, Kluwer, 1992, 31–41.

Krämer, L., *EC Treaty and Environmental Law*, London, Sweet & Maxwell, 1995.

Leppä, S., 'Control of Harm to the Environment and the United Nations Crime Prevention and Criminal Justice Programme', in Albrecht, H.J. and Leppä, S. (eds.), *Criminal Law and the Environment*, Helsinki, HEUNI, 1992, 89–92.

Meyer, J., Dessecker, A. and Smettan, J. (eds.), *Gewinnabschöpfung bei Betäubungsmitteldelikten*, Wiesbaden, Bundeskriminalamt, 1989.

Ogus, A., 'Legal Goals and Financial Institutions: Corrective Taxes and other Instruments', *Modern Law Review*, 1998, volume 61.

Sevenster, H.G., 'Milieustrafrecht in EEG-verband. Het Europa van de milieucrimineel', in Faure, M., Oudijk, J. en Schaffmeister, D. (eds.), *Zorgen van heden. Opstellen over het milieustrafrecht in theorie en praktijk*, Gouda Quint, 1991, 409–459.

Van den Wyngaert, Ch. (ed.), *Criminal Procedure Systems in the European Community*, London, Butterworths, 1993.

Van den Wyngaert, Ch. and Stessens, G. (eds.), *International Criminal Law. A Collection of International and European Instruments*, The Hague, Kluwer Law International, 1996.

Van der Landen, D., 'Naar een GeUNIEficeerd strafrecht?', *Delikt en Delinkwent*, 1994, 921–939.

X, International Review of Penal Law, 1994, 47–53.

ANNEX 1: QUESTIONNAIRE

IMPEL *AD HOC* WORKING GROUP ON CRIMINAL PROSECUTION TOPICS

1. Criminal liability of corporations for environmental offences

(a) Can companies be held criminally liable for environmental offences?
(b) Can directors and/or managers be held criminally liable as well as the company?
(c) How is liability constructed in practice against a company? For instance, is it necessary to prove liability against an individual employee who has caused the pollution incident?
(d) If your answer to (a) is no, in what other ways may companies be punished for a pollution incident?
(e) If your answer to (a) is no, can you explain any drawbacks you can identify in your system caused by an inability to prosecute companies?

2. The role of enforcing bodies and individuals in connection with environmental offences

(a) Identify the enforcing bodies which may bring criminal prosecutions for environmental offences in your country.
(b) Can individuals also bring criminal prosecutions for environmental offences?
(c) Is the permission of the public prosecutor or similar authority required before a prosecution is commenced?
(d) If your answer to (b) is yes, please describe how individuals may bring a prosecution procedurally. Can you identify any advantages or disadvantages to the system you describe which allows access to the courts to individuals to prosecute?
(e) If your answer to (b) is no, are there any ways that an individual can effect or

participate in a public prosecution?
(f) Does the fact that certain bodies and individuals bring criminal prosecutions for environmental offences affect the role of the public prosecutor?
(g) What is the role of the enforcing bodies, individuals, police and public prosecutor and others in the investigation of environmental crime?
(h) What do you consider enforcing bodies and individuals contribute to the proper regulation and enforcement of environmental law in your country?

3. Criminal penalties

(a) Please describe the criminal sanctions that may be applied to those found liable for environmental offences.
(b) Which sanctions in your experience are most commonly applied? Please give examples of levels of fines/prison sentences.
(c) Which sanctions in your experience are very rarely applied, if at all?
(d) What reasons would you give for the answers given to (b) and (c)?
(e) Are criminal sanctions imposed by the Court, the public prosecutor or by some other tribunal or authority?

4. Administrative Sanctions

In some countries provision exists for fines and other sanctions to be levied without recourse to the courts, either by way of fixed penalties or administrative fines.

(a) Can administrative bodies impose fines without criminal proceedings?
(b) Would you categorise the imposition of such fines as a purely administrative sanction of a criminal sanction?
(c) If your country has civil or administrative sanctions please explain the relationship to criminal sanctions. Are civil or administrative sanctions equivalent in scale and effect to criminal sanctions?
(d) How frequently are such fines imposed?
(e) To what extent does the fact that enforcing bodies may impose such fines contribute to the proper regulation and enforcement of environmental law in your country?

5. Existence of Instruments which Prohibit individuals from carrying out a similar activity

(a) Is there provision in your country's environmental legislation for an instrument of notice which may be served on an individual prohibiting the carrying on of a particular activity of a profession in the future?
(b) If your answer to (a) is yes, is the instrument or notice a criminal sanction or is it an administrative tool used by administrative bodies?
(c) Is the notice served by the Court, the public prosecutor or similar authority to the administrative body?

(d) Please describe the way in which, and the circumstances where, such an instrument or notice is used in practice in your country.
(e) How frequently are such instruments/notices used in your country?
(f) What is the practical effectiveness of this instrument as a deterrent given the possibility of an individual operating under cover of another company or legal entity?

6. Transfrontier pollution incidents

(a) Please describe any investigation of prosecution of specific incidents of transfrontier pollution that your country has experienced.
(b) When dealing with transfrontier pollution incidents, what particular problems did the investigating and prosecuting bodies face?
(c) In your experience, are their sufficient formal treaties or other arrangements between Member States to enable effective investigation and/or extradition of individual polluters in cases of transboundary incidents? Please explain any problems that you have experienced.

7. Criminal liability for environmental offences by public servants and public authorities

(a) Are civil servants and public authorities capable of being held criminally liable for environmental offences in your country?
(b) If the answer to (a) is 'no', in what other ways may such individuals and authorities be held liable for environmental offences?
(c) If the answer to (a) is 'yes', please give details of how the system works.
(d) If civil servants and public authorities may be held criminally liable for environmental offences, does this affect the way civil servants and public authorities conduct their affairs?

8. Miscellaneous

(a) In your experience do you find that administrative sanctions are as effective as a deterrent as criminal sanctions pursued through the Court system?
(b) As a general rule do you find that prosecution is initiated or an administrative sanction imposed for most breaches of your country's environmental legislation or is there tolerance for minor breaches i.e. technical breaches of a permit, which do not cause much environmental harm by administrative bodies, public prosecutors or government.
(c) What is the role, if any, of the intelligence services in environmental investigation? In your country is there cooperation between the intelligence services, the police and/or the body responsible for investigating an environmental incident? Can any information supplied by the intelligence services be used in criminal proceedings?

ANNEX 2: COUNTRY REPORTS

1. AUSTRIA

Respondent: Ms. Petra Smutny

1. Criminal liability of Corporations for Environmental Offences

(a) No.

(b) Yes.

(c) —

(d) There is the possibility to confiscate enrichments that are based on the illegal environmental offence.

2. The role of enforcing bodies and individuals in connection with environmental offences

(a) Police, administrative organs, environmentalists (NGO's), newspapers, political groups.

(b) Yes.

(c) No (at least not in the beginning of criminal prosecution).

(d) Criminal prosecution by individuals starts with a report to the police.

(e) —

(f) No.

(g) See answer to part III.

(h) There are frequent exchanges of experience, direct contribution is hard to ascertain but always immanent and shown by many amendments during the last years.

3. Criminal penalties

(a) Judicial sanctions are imprisonment of up to three years of fines of up to 360 day-fines (max. 1,82 mio. ATS).

(b) Most applied fines are from 60 up to 180 day-fines, all sentences to imprisonment are suspended on probation and from 3 up to 6 months.

(c) See answer to question 3b.

(d) In Austria the greatest merit of environmental criminal law lies within the effect on prevention. Sentences that are suspended on probation full fill this task better and for a longer term.

(e) Court.

4. Administrative Sanctions

(a) Yes.

(b) Administrative sanctions can also be penal provisions but there is a strict distinction between administrative penalty procedure and the criminal justice system.

(c) Administrative sanctions are not equivalent in scale but more often imposed because of less requirements.

(d) No information available. For further information please contact Dr. Gerhard Gödl, Amt der Steiermärkischen Landesregierung, 8011 Graz, Landhausgasse 7.

(e) To a large extent, but exact data are not available.

5. Existence of Instruments which Prohibit individuals from carrying out a similar activity

(a) No.

(b) —

(c) —

(d) —

(e) —

(f) —

6. Transfrontier pollution incidents

(a) For instance: great extended water-pollution of a river on the border to Slovenia. Both countries set investigation and prosecution activities.

(b) Public prosecutors complain that in some cases it was very hard to get essential information from neighbouring countries.

(c) See answer to question 6b.

7. Criminal liability for environmental offences by public servants and public authorities

(a) Yes.

(b) —

(c) Civil servants can either be prosecuted for committing an environmental crime and/or for abuse of authority.

(d) Information are not available.

8. Miscellaneous

(a) See answer to question 3d.

(b) No.

(c) No.

(d) Competent authority over investigation of international environmental offences has the Ministry of the Interior (Abt. II/10. NBZ Wien, IKPO-INTERPOL, 1090 Wien, Liechtenwerderplatz 5). All supplied information can be used in criminal proceedings.

2. BELGIUM

Respondent: Mrs. Anne-Marie Gepts

1. Criminal liability of Corporations for Environmental Offences

(a) Since the Liability of Legal Persons under Criminal Law Act of May 4th 1999 was introduced, a legal person can be held responsible under criminal law, with the exception however of the political legal persons such as the federal state, the regions, the communities, the provinces, the municipalities … and the Public Centres for Social Welfare.

(b) When the legal person is solely held responsible because of the action of an identified natural person, only the one who has committed the most serious error, can be sentenced. If the identified natural person has committed the error knowingly and wilfully, he can be sentenced together with the responsible legal person.

(c) A legal person is responsible under criminal law for criminal offences which are intrinsically related to the realization of its aim or the representation of its interests, or which, as shown by concrete circumstances, have been committed on its own behalf. In other words, the legislator has opted for a system in which it is assumed that the legal person can commit an error, can exhibit reprehensible behaviour and can be punished without the judge having to look in the legal person's organization for a natural person to blame. The concurrence of the responsibility of the legal person and the natural person mentioned under (b) – the legal person's responsibility being compromised solely because of the action of an identified natural person – doesn't depart from the basic principle that it's not necessary to identify a natural person in order to be able to sentence the legal person.

(d) Since the entry into force of the Act of May 4th 1999, a number of specific punishments were entered, applicable to the criminal offences committed by legal persons. In criminal and police matters, it involves the fine and the special confiscation. In addition to the aforesaid punishments, four punishments may be imposed, namely the publication or the circulation of the decision, the closure of one or more establishments, the prohibition of performing a work which is part of the company's object and finally the dissolution, however on a number of restrictive conditions. Administrative penalties and/or sanctions and/or compulsory measures can be imposed upon legal persons, too. Finally, the company may also be summoned to appear before the judge in interlocutory proceedings or before the civil court.

2. The role of enforcing bodies and individuals in connection with environmental offences

(a) The public prosecutions department is the only body which has the power to take criminal action against environmental offences.

(b) Individual persons can also prosecute, but only on the conditions provided under (d).

(c) In the cases mentioned under (b), no prior permission of the public prosecutions department or a similar authority is required.

(d) He who alleges to be injured by a criminal offence, can bring an action as a plaintiff claiming damages before the competent examining magistrate. The plaintiff claiming damages can also directly summon the suspect before the criminal court for cases coming within the competence of the criminal court.

(e) Doesn't apply in view of the answers given to the questions under (b) and (d).

(f) The possibilities in store for the plaintiff claiming damages to prosecute, have repercussions on the public prosecution department's powers in the sense that, after the judicial inquiry being closed by the examining magistrate, the public prosecutor only can claim the court sitting in camera to refer or to dismiss the case if there are sufficient respectively insufficient objections. At this stage, an amicable settlement or an abandonment of prosecution purely for opportunist reasons isn't possible any more.

(g) The establishment of environmental offences is done for the greater part by particular officials (control officers yet with judicial police power when establishing a criminal offence) and, on the other hand, by the ordinary police services acting in the capacity of their general establishment authority.

(h) Though both particular officials and ordinary police services act ex officio, the complaints of private individuals and environmental organizations, too, play an important part in environmental offences enforcement.

3. Criminal penalties

(a) As for the punishments which can be imposed on the legal person, we refer to what we said under point 1. (d). For natural persons, most environment laws contain an imprisonment and/or a fine, as well as additional measures such as the prohibition to run the establishment, the confiscation of the property gains, the confiscation of the waste and the packaging, the sentence to remove the waste materials which were illegally left behind or to pay back the costs for the removal of the waste materials, which can be pronounced in respect of legal persons also.

(b) The fine is the penal sanction which is most often pronounced. Prison sentences also are imposed, but to a clearly lesser extent and as a rule wholly or partially suspended. Depending on the gravity of the facts, fines are imposed of an average of 20,000 BF to 1,000,000 BF (whether or not suspended).

(c) The prohibition to run the establishment, the confiscation of the waste and the packaging, the execution of prescribed measures are sanctions which are rarely ordered. In the last few years, courts impose increasingly measures mentioned under (a), such as the removal of waste materials linked to a default fine, although one cannot call it a generalized tendency.

(d) The reason why mainly fines and (suspended) prison sentences are pronounced, is due to the fact that the environmental legislation provides for administrative sanctions which can be imposed immediately after the establishment of the environmental infringement by administrative authorities (see further under point 4). When the case is heard by the criminal judge, it is not infrequently found to be regularized.

(e) The criminal sanctions are imposed by the courts.

4. Administrative sanctions

(a) For a restricted number of environmental offences, mainly within the framework of the legislation on contamination by fertilizers (e.g. by not fulfilling the obligation to pay manure production levies, by discharging manure, by illegally dumping manure surpluses), the administrative authorities can impose administrative fines without say of the judicial authorities.

(b) So, administrative fines should be considered in the above context a purely administrative sanction, because they apply without prejudice to the applicable penal provisions.

(c) A whole series of compulsory measures exists, going from the imposition of oral or written warnings to the order to stop the activities, the sealing up of appliances, the closure of the establishment, the removal ex officio of waste materials at the expense of the offender, the return of the waste materials to the sending State,. ... If administrative measures are imposed in case of petty environmental offences, claiming additional penal sanctions in a court of justice generally becomes superfluous. In case of serious environmental offences, one opts for the simultaneous imposition of administrative and penal sanctions in order to guarantee a better environmental legislation enforcement.

(d) Administrative penalties are imposed for a number of offences enumerated by the law, mainly within the framework of the waste materials contamination act.

(e) In view of the restricted legal possibilities, the administrative penalty only contributes to a very small extent to environmental legislation enforcement. Another possibility is provided for for the public prosecutions department, which can request the perpetrator to pay a fixed sum of money (amicable settlement). The payment extinguishes the prosecution. More and more, amicable settlement is considered an important instrument for environmental legislation enforcement.

5. Existence of Instruments which prohibit individuals from carrying out a similar activity

(a) Environmental organizations meeting certain conditions, administrative authorities, inhabitants on behalf of the municipality, when the municipality doesn't take legal action, and the public prosecutor are authorized to bring an action for cessation before the Chairman of the Court of First Instance in case of manifest environmental offences or a serious threat for an environment infringement. In cases of urgency, the chairman of the court of first instance can, in interlocutory proceedings, give judgment by anticipation. Administrative authorities (burgomaster, environmental inspections, municipal environmental protection officers) also may impose administrative (compulsory) measures, such as clean-up measures, cessation of the activities, sealing up of appliances, closure of the establishment. The licensing authority can withdraw or suspend the licence.

(b) The measures mentioned first (which aren't penal sanctions) are pronounced by the Chairman of the Court of First Instance. On the other hand, the administrative (compulsory) measures are imposed by administrative authorities, generally control officers.

(c) See under (b).

(d) An environmental cessation action may be instituted to stop acts of which the execution has already begun or in view of imposing measures to prevent environmental damage, e.g. when a (legal) person intends to carry out an act which requires a licence, without having such a licence. Administrative (compulsory) measures will be imposed when infringements are established: as a rule, orders are given first and if they're not observed within a given term, farther-reaching measures will be taken (discontinuation activities, placing under seal, closure establishment).

(e) Especially environmental organizations and, to a lesser degree, inhabitants on behalf of the municipality make use of the environmental cessation action. Warnings (such as clean-up measures) are applied frequently; as a rule, the other measures or proceedings will only be imposed when the initial measures are not observed.

(f) Since the described means are aimed against certain acts, the circumstance that a person operates under cover of another company, generally hasn't many repercussions (except for organized crime cases) on the effectiveness of the measure. The problem is more likely to arise with the penal imputation of the infringements.

6. Transfrontier pollution incidents

(a) Most cross-border environmental cases relate to the illegal transfer of waste materials and to illegal dealing in threatened species of animals and plants. As in particular for the illegal transfer of waste materials, all kinds of documents (transportation documents, invoices, ...) are forged, mainly with regard to the origin, the destination and the nature of the waste. The criminals move their action field to better places as the authorities are close on their heels elsewhere: from the Netherlands to the Flemish Region, then to Brussels and the Walloon Region and they end up dumping illegally in Northern France. More than once they operate through a complicated network of companies, but with always the same persons on the head, with the sole intention of preventing the illegal waste flows circles from being uncovered. Generally the cases of illegal dealing in threatened species of animals and plants come to light as a result of customs inspections.

(b) As a rule in cross-border environment cases, not only the material infringement should be established, but also an investigation is to be carried out into the person responsible under criminal law for the infringement (such as sender and addressee of the waste materials and of the threatened species of animals and plants abroad). Either the investigation should be continued abroad by means of rogatory letters, or a transfer of proceedings request should be sent abroad. The specified proceedings thereto need to be followed, though they often take up a lot of time. As for the travel assignment, the execution depends on the consent of the foreign authorities, which sometimes is long in coming and often subject to certain conditions. States still hold on to much to their national sovereignty. In conclusion, public prosecutors need to come to clear agreements beforehand in prosecution matters, in order to prevent double prosecution or, on the contrary, to prevent someone from escaping prosecution where it is necessary.

(c) Most treaties let the execution of rogatory letters depend on certain conditions. Rogatory letters intended for a search of premises or a seizure, for example, will be carried out only for facts which may give rise to extradition (Benelux Treaty on Extradition). The Schengen Agreement, too, let the grantability of rogatory letters intended for a search of premises or a seizure be subject to the condition that the fact which is on the basis of the letters rogatory is punishable by a prison sentence to a maximum of at least six months. Infringements e.g. of the Washington Convention are punishable by a prison sentence of not more than three months. In a number of bilateral agreements, extradition and execution of letters rogatory are only possible for specified criminal offences. Environmental offences are not included in the limitative lists.

7. Criminal liability for environmental offences by public servants and public authorities

(a) Officials can be held liable under criminal law for environmental infringements. Legal persons governed by public law can be divided into public institutions and political legal persons. Except for the public centres for social welfare, public institutions are liable under criminal law. However, political legal persons such as the federal state, the regions, the communities, the provinces, the municipalities, ... , were extracted from the sphere of application of the liability under criminal law of legal persons.

(b) Doesn't apply.

(c) As already stated under (a), for political legal persons, it is necessary to find out by the agency of whom the administration has acted, who had power of decision inside the legal person, who had the power to stop the infringement; as for public institutions, the identified natural persons and/or the institution itself can be prosecuted.

(d) In former years, the attitude of the authorities towards the compliance with the environmental legislation was found to be far to lax. In the last few years, the tide turned, maybe as a result of a number of convictions and/or of the population's increasing awakening with regard to environmental issues.

8. Miscellaneous

(a) Administrative sanctions are as effective as criminal sanctions. Efficient environment preservation needs continuous interaction between administrative and penal sanctions; for that purpose, regular consultations between administrative and judicial authorities are highly important.

(b) There is no such thing as a systematic tolerance of certain environmental infringements. But on certain levels (and mainly on the municipal level, though there are vast differences from one municipality to another) a laxer attitude is noticeable. The establishment of environmental infringements, too, leaves a lot to be desired in places, for lack of on-site inspections. The environmental legislation know-how among regular police services is not satisfactory.

(c) The environmental administrations mainly have a control task; furthermore, they can impose administrative measures. When their controls lead them to establish an infringement, they are obliged to make a report, which they have to send to the public prosecutor. They chiefly render technical assistance to the public prosecutions department, the examining magistrate and the ordinary police services in punctual cases. Regular consultations are held as to that between the services concerned. The specialized services' technical know-how is frequently used in criminal proceedings.

3. DENMARK

Respondent: Marianne Christensen

1. Criminal liability of Corporations for Environmental Offences

(a) According to Danish law companies can be held criminally liable for environmental offences.

(b) As well as the company, directors and/or managers may in certain cases be held liable.

(c) Criminal liability for the company can be enforced also where it has not been proven that a specific employee has caused the incident, as long as it can be established that the company as such must be responsible regarding the incident.

(d) Not relevant according to the answer to a.

2. The role of enforcing bodies and individuals in connection with environmental offences

(a) The Prosecution service is the only competent authority.

(b) Individuals can not bring criminal prosecutions for environmental offences.

(c) Yes.

(d) Not relevant according to the answer to b.

(e) An individual can first of all report possible offences to the police and can furthermore contribute with his or her knowledge as a witness. An individual may also claim damages during the trial, if civil liability is in question.

(f) Not relevant according to the answer to b.

(g) The enforcing bodies are supposed to work in close co-operation with the police and the prosecution service in order to bring up necessary evidence and to provide technical assistance. As to the role of individuals see the answer to e.

(h) In my opinion you can not imagine enforcement of environmental law without the special enforcing bodies playing a very active role. Individuals are to some extent important too, as it is the case concerning any criminal investigation.

3. Criminal penalties

Special remarks

The rules are contained in section 110 of the Danish Environmental Protection Act (enclosed). Under subsection 1, in law and in practice, the main rule is that offenders are liable to a fine. Under circumstances described in subsection 2 the penalty may be detention or imprisonment for a maximum term of two years. Where violation gave rise to profits they are confiscated in accordance with section 110 subsection 5.

As mentioned above, the absolute main rule is the fine, possibly combined with a confiscation of profits. The intention of the legislator is of course that one should not benefit from environmental crime and this intention should form basis for the Court's fixing of the fine. It is, however, extremely difficult to assess whether this intention has been truly reflected in the fines. You cannot state that there is a firm practice in the Danish courts and there are very few decisions from the Supreme Court. Anyhow, I will describe the extremes and give an idea of the level where most of the fines lies and of the level of the combined sanctions, fines and confiscation.

As an indication I can refer to the following table on criminal cases from the Agency's latest report on environmental crime:

	Number of cases	**Number of fines**	**Detention/ imprisonment**	**Amount of fines (DKr)**	**Amount of confiscation (DKr)**
Agriculture	93: 61	60	—	302,000	—
	94: 99	96		390,000	
Industry	93: 81	75	1	1,017,000	648,000
	94: 70	65	1	1,427,000	1,423,000
Territorial waters	93: 46	45	—	86,000	200,000
	94: 45	41		60,000	0
Total	93: 188	180	1	1,400,000	848,000
	94: 214	202	1	1,874,000	1,423,000

The average fine in the area of agriculture was approx. 4,000 DKr. The average fine in the area on industry was 21,900 DKr.

Subsection 2 (detention/imprisonment) has been invoked in very few cases and the maximum penalty has been 40 days of detention. At present, there is a pending case where the prosecution wants to press for imprisonment. It is still too early to predict whether imprisonment actually will be the result and for how long.

It follows from the above that subsection 2 is very seldom applied. Furthermore, section 110b, on loss of right to carry out certain activities, has not yet been invoked due to the fact that it only entered into force last summer.

Criminal sanctions are as the main rule imposed by the Court. I refer to the response under 4.

4. Administrative Sanctions

Special remarks

I refer to section 110a. The agency is not in possession of information concerning possible cases. The issue, administrative fines, has been raised in connection with oil pollution at sea, but has not yet been decided.

I have no information as to answers to the specific questions.

5. Existence of Instruments which Prohibit individuals from carrying out a similar activity

Special remarks

I refer to section 110b and to the enclosed memo. There has to date not been reported any cases to the agency. It was expected during the drafting process that the annual number would be 10 or so.

6. Transfrontier pollution incidents

Special remarks

We have several cases of illegal transfrontier shipment of waste and oil pollution at sea.

7. Criminal liability for environmental offences by public servants and public authorities

(a) Yes, they can be held responsible.

(b) Not relevant according to the answer to a).

(c) The system works in a way comparable to the system concerning the liability of companies.

(d) Yes, I would think so.

8. Miscellaneous

(a) This will depend on the content of the administrative sanctions.

(b) The seriousness of the case will be reflected in the sanctions. Minor breaches will often be met with minor sanctions.

(c) The intelligence service will not normally play any role in environmental investigation. Anyhow, links between the relevant organizations could easily be established if necessary in a specific case.

Special remarks

Legislators intention is clearly that also breaches which could be characterized as formal without causing environmental harm should be prosecuted and fined. The level of fines as decided by the courts is influenced by the fact that an environmental crime was only formal.

The structure of the Criminal Justice System in Denmark

1. The Hierarchy of Courts

In Denmark penal cases are dealt with by the general courts. There exists a hierarchy of general courts, consisting of three levels. The first level is the district courts (byretterne). There are 82 district courts. The second level is the High Courts (Landsretterne), of which there are two. The Supreme Court (Højesteret) constitutes the third level.

The defendant normally stands trial at the district court, unless appearance for a jury in the High Court is specifically prescribed by the law. Appeal against judgements of district courts can normally be put forward to the High Courts, then acting as Courts of Appeal. Subsequently, appeals against the decisions of the High Courts (courts of appeal) can be put forward to the Supreme Court, always acting as Court of Appeal. However, an appeal to the Supreme Court is subject to special leave, which is in principle given only if the case is of general public importance. The leave is granted by the Board of Leaves, an independent board consisting of one judge of the Supreme Court, one judge of one of the High Courts, one judge of one of the district courts, one barrister (authorized to appear before the Supreme Court) and finally, one distinguished jurist, all of them appointed by the Crown.

Cases relating to a crime that may carry a sentence of imprisonment of 4 years or more, and cases concerning political offences – in so far the defendant has not pleaded guilty – will generally be tried before a High court as a court of first instance with the participation of a jury Appeals against sentences passed in a High Court as a court of first instance may be brought before the Supreme Court without a special leave from the Board of Leaves. However, the Supreme Court cannot give an opinion as to whether the evidence has been judged erroneously.

2. The Prosecution System

Formally the head of the prosecution service is the Minister of Justice (Justitsministeren).

The Minister has the political responsibility for the police and prosecution service. He prepares the laws and amendments of laws from Government concerning the police and prosecution system and presents them to the Parliament, and he is responsible for the necessary financial means, so that the police and prosecution system can perform their functions. He is in practice responsible for the appointment of all lawyers in the police and prosecution service, who are all civil servants. The highest placed of them are formally appointed by the Crown.

The Minister can give general instructions to the Director of Public Prosecutions and to the prosecution service as a whole, but does so very seldom, leaving that to the Director of Public Prosecutions with certain exceptions.

The Minister, by custom, does not interfere with the management of prosecutions in individual cases. However, decisions from the Director of Public Prosecutions can by complaint be brought before the Minister, for instance certain decisions to prosecute or not to prosecute. And in some cases, for instance concerning crimes against the State, such as espionage and treason, decisions to prosecute is always taken by the Minister.

The Director of Public Prosecutions (Rigsadvokaten) is in practice the supreme prosecuting authority for the country as a whole, and he is the organizational head of the prosecution service. He has two deputies and eight full-time and five part-time assistant lawyers attached to his office, all civil servants, appointed by the Crown or the Minister of Justice.

The Public Prosecutors refer cases which require special attention to the Director of Public Prosecutions. Likewise complaints against decisions by the Public Prosecutors, for instance to discharge a suspect or not to prosecute because of insufficient evidence, can be brought before him. He can order that a particular case be referred to him for review, and he can even direct that certain types of cases shall be so referred. He issues general directions to the Public Prosecutors and the local Chiefs of Police as well as specific information and instruction on matters of criminal law and procedure. He acts as adviser to the Minister of Justice on matters of a general nature, for instance concerning amendments of the penal law. He decides whether a High Court judgement shall be appealed to the Supreme Court, where he and his two deputies, as well as two of his full-time lawyers, appear as prosecutors in criminal cases.

Under the Director of Public Prosecutions there is a service of Public Prosecutors (statsadvokater):

There are six district Public Prosecutors. Each Public Prosecutor has one or two Deputies Public Prosecutors and several full-time and some part-time assistant lawyers.

In addition to the district Public Prosecutors there is a Special Public Prosecutor who in the country as a whole is responsible for investigating complicated or very large financial and economic crimes. He has three deputies and 14 full-time assistant lawyers and, as the only public prosecutor, a number of police investigators directly attached to his office.

In the most serious criminal cases the decision to prosecute or not to prosecute is made by the Public Prosecutor. He (or his deputies or assistant lawyers) also appears in cases tried before a jury in the High Courts and in all cases, where the High Courts function as Courts of Appeal.

The Chiefs of Police are under supervision by the district Public Prosecutors, and all their decisions concerning prosecutions can by complaint be brought before the Public Prosecutor. The Public Prosecutor can also without complaint change the decisions of the Chiefs of Police to prosecute or not to prosecute, and he can give general instructions in this respect. The Public Prosecutor also decides whether a district court judgement or decision shall be appealed to the High Court by the prosecution service.

Under the Public Prosecutors there are 53 police districts headed by Chiefs of Police (politimestre) and a separately organized Metropolitan Police for the City of Copenhagen, headed by a Police Director (politidirektør).

The Chiefs of Police and the police director are always lawyers. They have a deputy (also a lawyer) – the biggest police districts several deputies – and a number of assistant lawyers.

The Chiefs of Police (and the Police Director) have a double function: They are chiefs of the local police force, and in this capacity responsible also for the investigation of crimes. Besides that they and their deputies or assistants – all of them lawyers – represent the prosecution at the first level (i.e the district courts). They are responsible for initiating proceedings in all ordinary cases and always represent the prosecution in the district courts in such cases, also in cases when the indictment originates from the Public Prosecutor. In these capacities the Chiefs of Police and their legal staff are part of the public prosecution service.

Danish Environmental Protection Agency
Enforcement and Legislation Division
November 24, 1997
KDJ/7

Memo on New Danish rules on Enforcement of Environmental-Law

In the summer of 1997 the Danish Parliament adopted a number of rules on enforcement of environmental law, with a view to ensuring more law and order in the field of the environment.

The Danish system of approval of heavily polluting activities was introduced already in 1972, with the adoption of the first Danish Environmental Protection Act. In their decision whether polluting activities can be approved, the environmental authorities have so far only been able to base their evaluation on the production plant and intended production site of the plant. Aspects of pollution were regulated in terms laid down in the approval, and by notices of orders or prohibitions.

The operation of industry or other polluting activities did not require a special *personal* authorization or other evaluation of conduct. Thus, any owner of a company had a legal claim for environmental approval of his activities, provided they fulfilled the environmental requirements for production stipulated by the supervisory authority. The ability of the management to operate the activities was not included in the review of an application for environmental approval.

This procedure is changed with the new Environmental Protection Act in 1997. Briefly, the new enforcement rules introduced three new instruments:

Firstly, environmental responsibility has become a criterium for approval of new polluting activities. 'Loss of environmental responsibility' shall, thus, be included in the decision whether polluting activities can be approved or not. Environmental responsibility is lost when an individual or a company with decisive influence on the operation of the plant is previously convicted of gross violation of Danish environmental legislation, or has by court order been disqualified from operating polluting activities, or is indebted to the environmental authorities with substantial amounts pertaining to clean-up of pollution for which the person or company was responsible.

Environmental responsibility implies that if the responsible management is not found to be qualified to operate polluting activities, the environmental authorities may refuse to grant environmental approval or may lay down special approval terms. Such a procedure can be applied if the applicant in person or if members of the management of the applying company has lost his or their environmental responsibility, and should therefore be considered less able to operate the activity for which prosecution is sought.

Moreover, loss of environmental responsibility by the management of an existing approved plant may have the result that the environmental authority can lay down new approval terms, stipulate requirements for provision of security as a condition for upholding the approval, or decide that the approval shall be fully withdrawn and the plant be closed.

Secondly, the loss of environmental responsibility of a company is in the cases above linked directly to the management of the company, i.a. where the holder of the approval, members of the board or others having influence on the company, lose environmental responsibility. Environmental responsibility can also be lost, where individuals or companies who have in another connection lost environmental responsibility take over the company wholly or partly, or where individuals who have lost environmental responsibility join the group of persons responsible for the company.

The third new instrument is a new register listing the persons and companies who have lost environmental responsibility. The register was introduced in connection with the new set of rules under which environmental authorities may in their review of applications for approval of polluting activities attach importance to environmental responsibility. Such rules can only be fully applied if the authorities are informed of possible previous violations.

By operation of polluting activities, environmental legislation may be violated so grossly, that the person or company must be considered unable to operate polluting activities in a sound manner in the future. The new legislation therefore provides for a new instrument disqualifying the offender from operating polluting activities. The power to disqualify at the courts is now provided, and the rules supplement the administrative power to refuse or withdraw permits to operate polluting activities.

As will appear from the above, the new instruments reflect a marked strengthening in Denmark of procedures towards individuals and companies speculating in breaches of environmental law-offenders with previous records, and kitefliers. Enforcement of the new rules is expected to ensure more law and order in the field of the environment and to limit the number of major pollution cases in Denmark. The new instruments are also expected to strengthen enforcement of the polluter pays principle in the future.

4. FINLAND

Respondent: Mr. Matti Nissinen

1. Criminal liability of Corporations for Environmental Offences

(a) Yes, on the basis of Finnish Penal Code (PC), Chapter 9, Sections 1–9 and Chapter 48, Section 9. However, liability is not applied to crimes committed by legal persons in the exercise of public authority (PC 9:1,2).

(b) Yes

(c) To establish liability of corporation it has to be proven either that someone on the managerial level is guilty or that in the organisation's activity due diligence and caution has not been exercised to prevent the crime (PC 9:2,1). So it is possible to punish a company even if the individual – an employee – who has caused the pollution incident remains unidentified (anonymous guilt) or – when being identified – in not prosecuted of sentenced, for instance because of death or limitation of criminal proceedings.

(d) (Answered: yes)

(e) (Answered: yes)

2. The role of enforcing bodies and individuals in connection with environmental offences

(a) Only public prosecutors can bring criminal prosecutions in environmental as well as in other kinds of offences. However, if quite exceptionally being considered as the plaintiff of the crime in question, also enforcing bodies can bring criminal prosecutions complying with the rules explained below (c).

(b) Only in the case that being considered as the plaintiff; for instance while being the owner of the land of other property which was polluted.

(c) No special 'permission' is required, but an individual (or enforcing bodies) can bring criminal prosecutions only after the public prosecutor has notified that he is not going to bring criminal prosecutions in the offence (The criminal Procedure Act CPA, 1:14).

(d) The procedure is very similar to the 'normal' criminal procedure, that is, when a public prosecutor is involved. Even then the investigation is taken care by the police and the case is brought before the court by filing a complaint (an application for a summons) (CPA 7:1). These cases are rare and even more rarely they lead to sentencing.

(e) (Answered: yes)

(f) It has no affect.

(g) Police is in charge of the investigation. Investigations are directed by a commanding police officer, normally a criminal inspector. Public prosecutor may consult the police investigators, issue instructions and orders on additional investigations etc.
Enforcing bodies can assist the investigation by giving background information for instance on the chemical properties of the waste involved.
Furthermore, it's the statutory duty of the enforcing bodies to oversee that the environmental laws are complied with.

(h) Most environmental cases are various minor offences. They are taken care with administrative means by enforcing bodies. Individuals have exposed some environmental crimes to police and to environmental bodies.

3. Criminal penalties

(a) Imprisonment, day-fines and petty fines can be applied. All punishment stipulations prescribe the punishment for the offence in question and also the maximum and the minimum are always mentioned. Also corporate liability is possible.

(b) Usually day-fines are applied. They are imposed as a certain number of days (from 1 to 120) at a certain sum each day. the size of the sum depends on the monthly income and assets of the offender. The average amount on day fines in environmental is perhaps about 20–30. Unpaid day-fines can be converted into imprisonment.

(c) Imprisonment is rather rarely applied – but it is applied, if necessary.

(d) The quality on the offences explains the selection of the punishment.

4. Administrative Sanctions

(a) No, they can not.

(b) (Not imposed)

(c) Administrative sanctions – for instance conditional imposition of a fine (which is not day-fine but a fixed amount can be used, when they are based on a proper administrative decision in order to strengthen what has been ordered, for instance the order to stop the pollution. These sanctions are effective because they are fast to use and big enough.

(d) There are no statistics available. They are used often.

(e) (In the questionnaire: f) It is a significant contribution to the proper regulation and enforcement.

5. Existence of Instruments which Prohibit individuals from carrying out a similar activity

(a) Yes.

(b) In principle: prohibition orders are possible in the form of 'prohibition exercising a business'.

(c) This prohibition order is a criminal side sanction.

(d) It is imposed by criminal court and requested by the public prosecutor.

(e) It has not been used due to an environmental crime.

(f) If been used, it would be rather effective; monitoring is still needed in order to prohibit the possibility to use undercover of another company or person.

6. Transfrontier pollution incidents

(a) I only know one case. A river flowing from Finland to Russia was polluted by a Finnish cardboard factory. The two directors of the factory were charged and sentenced (25 and 22 day-fines). The fact, that the case had thin 'transfrontier' qualification caused no special problems to investigation of prosecution. the Russian authorities were not involved in the proceedings.

(b) However, something should be done with the cases, when the spillage from a ship has been run into the sea.

(c) (see b) The MARPOL-convention doesn't authorize to stop the ship on the open sea – so the investigation is delayed.

7. Criminal liability for environmental offences by public servants and public authorities

(a) Yes they are.

(b) (Answered: yes.)

(c) There have been a few cases, when a civil servant representing an administrative body has been sentenced together with some persons representing the company, because due diligence has not been exercised when supervising the activity on the company in question. In those cases the police has reported suspicions about insufficient supervision aroused by it's own observations.

(d) I think that there is not a direct effect. Maybe the idea of responsibility is taken even more seriously.

8. Miscellaneous

(a) They are very difficult to compare or to measure. Maybe the publicity linked with the cases brought to the court has a special significance here (bad PR).

(b) There is – and there should be – a certain tolerance when for instance technical breaches of a permit is in question.

(c) There has not been any role of the intelligence in environmental investigation so far.

5. FRANCE

Respondent: Pof; Doctor Marcel Bayle, Directeur du CREOP (Centre de Recherches sur l'Entreprise, les Organisations et le Patrimoine), Limoges University.

1. Criminal liability of Corporations for Environmental Offences

(a) Can companies be held criminally liable for environmental offences?

Yes, since the new Penal Code 1994, article 121–2.

However: liability is not applied to offences committed by the French State.

Liability is not general for the local public authorities: they are only liable for offences committed in the exercise of activities that they could delegate to private enterprises.

Liability is not general for the corporations. They are liable only for the offences when the text which gives the provision indicates that this liability is possible. In practice, most of the environmental offences are previous by texts witch make this kind of provision. Now, this liability is quite general in environmental penal law.

(b) Can directors and/or managers be held criminally liable as well as the company?

Yes, article 121–2,§ 3 penal code: Criminal liability of Corporations don't inhibit from prosecute natural persons whether they are authors or accomplices of the same facts. However, since the law N° 2000–647 (10/7/2000), an important exception exists. The fourth paragraph of article 121–3 penal code, added by this law, exonerate the managers when their imprudence or their carelessness is only an indirect cause of the offence. It is only in case of personal characterized fault, or in case of personal evident lapse from duty about security or caution, that they may be held criminally liable for offences, especially environmental offences of personal characterized fault, or in case of personal evident lapse from a duty about security or caution, that they may be held criminally liable for offences, especially environmental offences

Please look at answer 7d).

(c) How is liability constructed in practice against a company? For instance, is it necessary to prove liability against an individual employee who has caused the pollution incident?

This liability is specific, even if it is easier proving liability against the managerial level. In this case, of course, it is possible to punish the company; but it is possible even whether the individual who has caused the pollution incident remains unidentified or, when being identified, is not prosecuted of sentenced, for instance because of limitation of criminal proceedings. To punish the company, it's enough to prove that in the organisation's activity due diligence and caution has not been exercised to prevent the crime

(d) (Answered: yes)

(e) (Answered: yes)

2. The role of enforcing bodies and individuals in connection with environmental offences

(a) Identify the enforcing bodies which may bring criminal prosecutions for environmental offences in your country.

Sticto sensu, only the public prosecutor and a specific administration (la DDAF: Direction Départementale de l'Agriculture et des Forêts) which is able to prosecute directly lawbreakers about two topics. First: fishing offences (article L 437–15 code rural), and second: forest offences in public forests, including hunting offences in these public forests (articles L. 153–1 to L. 153–10 code forestier).

Lato sensu, the French State through its various administrations, especially DDAF for others offences, DIREN (Direction Régionale de l'Environnement), DRIRE (Direction Régionale de l'Industrie et de la Recherche), CSP (Conseil Supérieur de la Pêche), ONCFS (Office National de la Chasse et de la Faune Sauvage). These offices are capable in the investigation of environmental crime. And many public legal persons are allowed to sue for damages the offender with the rules explained below for individuals (b). These public legal persons are: ADEME (Agence de l'environnement et de la maîtrise de l'énergie),, le «Conservatoire de l'espace littoral et des rivages lacustres», «les agences de l'eau» (water agencies),and so on.

(b) Can individuals also bring criminal prosecutions for environmental offences?

Yes, but not really by themselves. They are aloud to lodge a complaint against a company or against an individual, but they have to require the public prosecutor to bring criminal prosecutions for environmental offences. The individual is not exercising the public action, but he is obliging the judicial system to exercise the public action, even if this individual seems simply bringing his civil law suit before the criminal court.

(c) Is the permission of the public prosecutor or similar authority required before a prosecution is commenced?

No. Most certainly, the principle is that the action of the public prosecutor is required before a prosecution is commenced; but an important exception exists: each victim is able to lodge a special complaint ('la plainte avec constitution de partie civile'). This complaint is receipt by the coroner. This special victim's complaint obliges to bring the criminal prosecution, if the occurrences can receipt a penal qualification. It is not specific for environmental offences: these general rules are given by art. 85 to 91 CPP (Penal Proceedings Code). It is possible even if the public prosecutor has not notified that he is not going to bring criminal prosecutions in the offence.

(d) If your answer to (b) is yes, please describe how individuals may bring a prosecution procedurally. Can you identify any advantages or disadvantages to the system you describe which allows access to the courts to individuals to prosecute?

The victim, individual or NGOs, is able to register her special complaint near the coroner; but she has to deposit an amount in the court's secretary, amount fixed by the coroner. This system is justified by the risk of misuse. If the person who makes this special complaint can't make her opponent condemned, she loses this amount. It's a good guaranty against misuses.

The important advantage of this system is to bring more efficient the environmental protection. Victims, individuals or NGOs, become the watchmen (please look at answer: h).

If your answer to (b) is no, are there any ways that an individual can effect or participate in a public prosecution?

(Answered: yes)

(f) Does the fact that certain bodies and individuals bring criminal prosecutions for environmental offences affect the role of the public prosecutor?

No, because the public prosecutor is free to prosecute or not, according to his ethic; but some members of the 'Parquet' say that they are a little vexed in front of the NGOs tendency to do the 'plainte avec constitution de partie civile', when they (members of the 'Parquet') don't wish to prosecute !

What is the role of the enforcing bodies, individuals, police and public prosecutor and others in the investigation of environmental crime?

First, the contribution of administrative agencies is highly important to prevent damages. These agencies give advises, injunctions and, when it's usefull, they give an order: if the enterprise which is offending, don't realise the task to close the pollution or more generally the environmental damage, some enforcing bodies are able to pronounce an 'astreinte'. It's an amount, kind of conditional fine, witch is to be paid if the injunction is not efficient.

Second, in the investigation of environmental crime, enforcing bodies, of course, provide important technical informations to the public prosecution system. They help the polices to establish the offence. But, there is a dark number of the environmental offences. A kind of selection is done by the enforcing bodies, then by the public prosecutor. Few environmental offenders are prosecuted criminaly.

Third, the role of the victims, particularly of the NGOs whitch are victims, is important (answer h).

(h) What do you consider enforcing bodies and individuals contribute to the proper regulation and enforcement of environmental law in your country?

From a sociological point of view, the main phenomenon, since 1980 up to now, is in the multiplication of the environmental club's actions., as victims of the environmental offense, doing the 'plainte avec constitution de partie civile'. Especially fishers clubs, ornithological clubs, and NGOs, especially the big federation of environmental associations FNE (France Nature Environnement) made and make many special complaint. It seems that this phenomenon is strengthening the deterrent aspect of the penal environmental law. It discourages a part of environmental law breakers. The public awareness of environmental issues is growing and reaches a good level; so this system seems good.

3. Criminal penalties

(a) Please describe the criminal sanctions that may be applied to those found liable for environmental offences.

Some principles:

- Only is settled the maximum of the fine or imprisonment in the codes. The judge is able to settle freely down to one euro or one day imprisonment.
- In case of second offense ('récidive'), fines and imprisonment incured are multiplied by two.
- Fines for legal persons are the same than for individuals but multiplied by five.

There are many provisions. One is marginal: it is the ecological terrorism. One of the more classical is water pollution and the text most commonly applied is article L.432–2 code de l'environnement. In this case, the applicable sanction for individuals offenders is two years imprisonment and a fine, up to 18,000 euros. In the same case, but for legal persons, it is a fine up to 90,000 euros and various sanctions mentionned at article 131–39 pénal code. These sanctions, reserved for legal entities, are never applied in practice.

Criminal sanction provided for in legislation	**Sanctions most commonly applied**	**Examples**	**Rarely applied sanctions**
Ecological terrorism (art. 421–2 penal code): * imprisonment up to 15 years (life imprisonment if a victim is dead) * fine 225 000 euros (750 000 euros if a victim is dead) Others offences: * imprisonment up to 2 years * fines for natural persons: sometimes up to 75,000 euros (example art L. 216–6 code environnement) Fines for legal persons: * the same fines multiplied by 5.	Fines	In case of serious water pollution by an individual, 450 euros and one month suspended sentence are very possible.	Imprisonment without remission.

(b) Which sanctions in your experience are most commonly applied? Please give examples of levels of fines/prison sentences.

Fines

For instance, for violation of a ban about hunting, the individual offender can be probably sentenced to 1500 euros and 3 month suspended sentence.

Other example: a big company, lawbreaker in polluting water, can be sentenced to 3000 euros, that is nothing for her.

The French system of fines multiplicated by five for legal entities is not just. This amount is much for a very little SARL, and it's nothing for a big trust. A percentage of the company's turnover would be justified (for instance five per cent).

(c) Which sanctions in your experience are very rarely applied, if at all?
- For individuals: imprisonment without remission.
- For legal entities: the sanctions of article 131–39 penal code; for instance, closure of the polluting factory, confiscate the things produced in the polluting way, prohibition of the exercise of an activity.

(d) What reasons would you give for the answers given to (b) and (c)?

Mainly social reasons: trade-unions are set themselves against that kind of sanctions, in spite of their deterrent properties.

And a few judges are specialists of environmental law. Some of them have a kind of respect for white-collar offenders.

(e) Are criminal sanctions imposed by the Court, the public prosecutor or by some other tribunal or authority?
Criminal sanctions can only be imposed by the court.

4. Administrative Sanctions

In some countries provision exists for fines and other sanctions to be levied without recourse to the courts, either by way of fixed penalties or administrative fines.

(a) Can administrative bodies impose fines without criminal proceedings?

Yes, some of them, which ask to the main state representative in the district ('préfet') to impose a fine in some cases, for instance, for classified installations ('installations classes', article 514–1 code de l'environnement). Others systems of administrative fines exist under the authority of the minister in charge of environment, for instance to deal with problems of wastes (article L. 541–26 code de l'environnement).

(b) Would you categorise the imposition of such fines as a purely administrative sanction of a criminal sanction?
In these examples, fines are purely administrative sanction, without any interference of a judge or a criminal court.
If your country has civil or administrative sanctions please explain the relationship to criminal sanctions. Are civil or administrative sanctions equivalent in scale and effect to criminal sanctions?

This relationship is simple: often, the reports ('procès-verbaux') deposed by the enforcing body near the public prosecutor are not followed by a prosecution: the prosecutor don't prosecute! So, in many cases, administrative sanctions are more efficient than the penal way. And if the offender don't respect the administrative sanction, he is offending and a criminal prosecution becomes probable.

Civil sanctions, often associated with criminal sanctions, are not equivalent in scale and effect to these criminal sanctions. They compensate, they don't punish.

Administrative sanctions can be deterrent for small offenders.

(d) How frequently are such fines imposed?

Not uncommon.

(e) To what extent does the fact that enforcing bodies may impose such fines contribute to the proper regulation and enforcement of environmental law in your country?

It is really efficient, but because the criminal system is present in watermark to strength the administrative system. The disrespect of the administrative sanction is a criminal offence and, in that case, the public prosecutor prosecutes !

5. Existence of Instruments which Prohibit individuals from carrying out a similar activity

(a) Is there provision in your country's environmental legislation for an instrument of notice which may be served on an individual prohibiting the carrying on of a particular activity of a profession in the future?

In the criminal way, yes. This instrument's name is 'casier judiciaire'. It notices the convictions for each individual and for each legal person.

In the administrative way, not really. Most certainly, each administration notices the sanctions she pronounced, and, in some cases, she is allowed to refuse for instance a new permission of installation for the persons she sanctioned. But it's easy to make a new company to make this activity.

(b) If your answer to (a) is yes, is the instrument or notice a criminal sanction or is it an administrative tool used by administrative bodies?

It ('le casier judiciaire') is a penal tool ! For instance, if the offender is forbidden to exercise a commercial activity during five years, this notice is efficient for individuals. If they disrespect this personal prohibition, they are offending gravely. For legal persons, it's not really efficient, of course.

(c) Is the notice served by the Court, the public prosecutor or similar authority to the administrative body?

Yes. Before getting a new permission of activity, especially in commercial business, the person who asks the registration in the account-book has to present an extract of this notice ('extrait de casier judiciaire'). Sometimes, this system is used for getting a new permission of activity (installations classées pour la protection de l'environnement).

(d) Please describe the way in which, and the circumstances where, such an instrument or notice is used in practice in your country.

There is no automatic connexion between the 'casier judiciaire' and the enforcing bodies. But, when a new registration is applied, the person who asks for has to give the extract of her notice.

(e) How frequently are such instruments/notices used in your country?

It is systematic for a new registration in the account-book; it is occasional for new permissions of activities, when the persons are already registered on the account-book.

(f) What is the practical effectiveness of this instrument as a deterrent given the possibility of an individual operating under cover of another company or legal entity?

It's easy to make a new legal person to practise an activity in spite of a forfeiture.

6. Transfrontier pollution incidents

(a) Please describe any investigation of prosecution of specific incidents of transfrontier pollution that your country has experienced.

France has experienced some problems with Switzerland (pollution of Léman Lake water), with Belgium, Luxemburg, Germany, Spain about high risks (nuclear, chemical, forest fires). But in these cases, it seems that it were not the penal aspects witch were considered like important. Conventions of mutual aid were ratified (with Spain: 1959; with Luxembourg: 1962; with Germany: 1977; with Belgium: 1981), a specific convention was ratified to protect Léman Lake waters (1977), and another to prevent these waters against phosphates (Décret 89–215, 10/4/1989).

But these conventions are not penal conventions: they are mainly turned to civil protection.

(b) When dealing with transfrontier pollution incidents, what particular problems did the investigating and prosecuting bodies face?

Generally, cooperation between neighbouring states is good.

(c) In your experience, are their sufficient formal treaties or other arrangements between Member States to enable effective investigation and/or extradition of individual polluters in cases of transboundary incidents? Please explain any problems that you have experienced.

(d)

Description of transfrontier pollution incidents	Particular problems	Are formal treaties sufficient?
Water pollution cases with Switzerland (Lac Léman). Conventions about high risks with Spain, Luxembourg, Germany, Belgium.	Generally, cooperation between neighbouring states is good.	No because they don't include enough criminal aspects.

7. Criminal liability for environmental offences by public servants and public authorities

(a) Are civil servants and public authorities capable of being held criminally liable for environmental offences in your country?

In practice: no. Theoretically:Yes. There is no immunity for civil servants or public authorities. So they are capable of being held criminally liable for all their offences. But in practice, it's not an offence to give a bad advice or to commit an error in the administrative function, even if it is contributing to cause a pollution. Only in case of corruption, complicity or incitement of a civil servant, this criminal liability could be brought. In practice, it's marginal.

(b) If the answer to (a) is 'no', in what other ways may such individuals and authorities be held liable for environmental offences?
Corruption, complicity or incitement by a civil servant. But look at the answer N°1 about liability of legal persons, especially local public authorities: they are liable for offences committed on occasion of activities that they could delegate to private enterprises.

(c) If the answer to (a) is 'yes', please give details of how the system works.

(Answered: no)

(d) If civil servants and public authorities may be held criminally liable for environmental offences, does this affect the way civil servants and public authorities conduct their affairs?

Not for civil servants.

For legal public persons, the local councillors were disquiet until July 2000, when a new penal law, about indirect causality, brought them appeasement. Henceforth, it's only in case of personal characterized fault, or in case of personal evident lapse from duty about security or caution, that they may be held criminally liable for offences, especially environmental offences (article 121–3 penal code). Before this text, some local councillors and mayors refused to stand again as candidates in the elections, because of the risk of personal criminal liability.

8. Miscellaneous

(a) In your experience do you find that administrative sanctions are as effective as criminal sanctions pursued through the Court system as a deterrent?

No.

Most certainly, some administrative sanctions are really efficient as we explained it, but because the criminal system is present in watermark to strength the administrative system.

To make deterrent, we think that the risk of imprisonment, for managers of private enterprises, is more efficient, especially when they are convicted and are given a some month imprisonment suspended sentence. They don't make a second offence. But this way is marginal in France, and criminal liability of legal persons is substituted for criminal liability of managers.

(b) As a general rule do you find that a prosecution or an administrative sanction is imposed for most breaches of your country's environmental legislation or is there a tolerance of minor breaches i.e. technical breaches of a permit, which do not cause much environmental harm by administrative bodies, public prosecutors or government.

There is a tolerance of minor breaches for enterprises and their managers, not for individual offenders in the fields of fishing, hunting, or cruel behaviour against animals, and not for taggers. Most generally, there is a great tolerance in the field of economy, even in some cases of main environmental offenses.

(c) What is the role, if any, of the intelligence services in environmental investigation? In your country is there cooperation between the intelligence services, the police and/or the body responsible for investigating an environmental incident? Can any information supplied by the intelligence services be used in criminal proceedings?

No role except in the marginal field of ecological terrorism.

6. GERMANY

Respondent: Ms Eckhard Meyer-Rutz

1. Criminal liability of Corporations for Environmental Offences

(a) No; but non-penal fines can be imposed on corporations according to the Act on Administrative Regulatory Offences ('Gesetz über Ordnungswidrigkeiten').

(b) If the director/managers are criminally liable the corporation can be held liable as stated in (a), too.

(c) The pertinent provision of the Act on Administrative Regulatory Offences ('Gesetz über Ordnungswidrigkeiten') requires, inter alia, that a leading representative (as defined) of a legal person or another company or association commits a crime or an administrative regulatory offence ('Ordnungswidrigkeit') either in violation of a duty imposed on this legal person etc., or by which the legal person has been or should be enriched. The reference to an administrative regulatory offence includes the case where duties of supervision in relation to the prevention of a crime or administrative regulatory offence have been violated by such a leading representative and thereby alleviated the commission of such a crime or offence by a subordinate person. It is not necessary to identify the responsible representative as such if it can be established that at least one of such representatives has committed a pertinent crime or administrative regulatory offence.

(d) See (a)–(c)

(e) One of the main drawbacks/difficulties in investigation is to find out and to proof the responsibilities for specific actions in big companies. Currently some German politicians speak up for the criminal liability of corporations in general. See (a)- (c) as well.

2. The role of enforcing bodies and individuals in connection with environmental offences

(a) The right to bring action before a court rests with the public prosecutor (with some exceptions for the victim mentioned later). But the preliminary investigations are conducted and coordinated chiefly by a number of police forces and other authorities (under the supervision of the public prosecutor, see answer g):
- Police stations/headquarters (State authorities): investigation with specialized departments for environmental crimes, sometimes additional tasks e.g. in some States monitoring of waste shipments
- Federal Bureau of Investigation: focal point for national and international investigations concerning environmental crime, intelligence work/exchange of information; co-ordination and support in foreign criminal investigations, own investigations in cases of special interest, development of counteractive measures, membership in INTERPOL Working Parties
- State/Länder Bureaux of Investigation: mainly co-ordinating activities
- Water Police (State authority): investigations on larger rivers and in harbours
- Federal Border Police: investigations at territorial seas and within the Exclusive Economic Zone, investigations on sites owned by the Federal Railway
- Customs (federal authority): monitoring the import and export of goods, including related criminal investigations
- Mining Authorities (State authority): (not as a main task) criminal investigations on mining sites

(b) No, except in cases mentioned under (e).

(c) /

(d) /

(e) The individual victim of an environmental offence, i.e. anybody whose individual rights have been infringed, can participate in the criminal proceedings; the Code of Criminal Procedure confers on him certain rights in this respect. He cannot appear in court as a joint plaintiff, though. In addition a victim is granted a special legal remedy, i.e. a complaint, ('Beschwerde') against a decision of the public prosecutor not to prosecute.

(f) N/A

(g) The investigations are formally led by the public prosecutor, the police are obliged to support the public prosecutor. Individuals and enforcing bodies can be questioned by the public prosecutor. But specialized police units have as a rule more experience and expertise than the public prosecutor, thus in practice they often start the investigation and advise the public prosecutor.

(h) The role of environmental administrative authorities is important. They can often give decisive information on the administrative legal situation. These authorities, in addition also specialized bodies, provide technical and scientific assistance. The role of individuals seems to lie with the discovering of and reporting possible offences to the authorities.

3. Criminal penalties

(a) The main sanctions for criminal offences are imprisonment and (criminal) fines. In addition the following sanctions and measures may be applied: confiscation of instruments and proceeds (e.g. for saving of expenditures), ban on driving, revocation of drivers's licence. The relevant sanction in case of an administrative regulatory offence is a non-penal fine (which shall also cover the confiscation of proceeds); confiscation of instruments is possible if expressly permitted by law. This is usually the case in relation to environmental administrative regulatory offences.

(b) In criminal cases (criminal) fines are most commonly applied; in the case of administrative regulatory offences the imposition of non-penal monetary sanctions is the legal rule (e.g. EUR 10,000).

(c) Imprisonment is rarely imposed, in addition in most cases of imprisonment up to two years probation is granted.

(d) Most cases are of a minor nature, and, in addition, most offenders are first time offenders. A prolongation of proceedings in cases proceedings in cases of a complex nature may also contribute to lower sentences.

(e) Criminal sanctions are exclusively imposed by the courts. The public prosecutor may together with the court impose measures of amendment ('Auflagen und Weisungen') instead of a criminal sanction for minor offences, cf. Paragraph 153a Code of Criminal Procedure.

4. Administrative sanctions

(a) Yes; the Act on administrative regulatory offences provides its own rules on proceedings; usually they are simpler than the rules of criminal procedure, which, however, are partially applicable.

(b) Fines imposed by an administrative authority are administrative (penal) sanctions. The law determines a clear borderline between criminal and administrative sanctions. The assessment of this borderline by the legislative may change over the years.

A criminal offence carries as main sanctions imprisonment ('Freiheitsstrafe') or (criminal) fines ('Geldstrafe') to be imposed by a court.

An administrative regulatory offence ('Ordnungswidrigkeit'; 'Bußgeldtatbestand') carries as the main sanction a non-penal fine ('Geldbuße'), usually imposed in the first instance by an administrative authority.

(c) Cf. answer to (b). The non-payment of administrative fines ('Geldbuße') can be enforced by coercive detention ('Erzwingungshaft') which is different from imprisonment.

Administrative fines may be comparable in scale and effect to criminal fines. The most important environmental statutes provide for fines of up to 50,000 EUR. The law also provides, that the fines shall exceed all financial gains obtained by the perpetrator (Cf. Paragraph 17 (4) of the Act on Administrative Regulatory Offences). Criminal fines may be as high as 180,000 EUR.

(d) Very common.

(e) Important contribution to the enforcement of the law.

5. Existence of Instruments which Prohibit individuals form carrying out a similar activity

(a) Yes; e.g. a ban on a professional activity (based on the Criminal or the Trade or Industrial Code ['Gewerbeordnung']). Relevant are also measures whereby the operation of certain installations is prohibited.

(b) It may be a criminal measure (even imposed provisionally already during the investigations or proceedings), an administrative decision, or both.

(c) According to the nature of the measure, it is imposed by the court or the competent administrative authority.

(d) A criminal and an administrative ban is in practice usually imposed only in serious cases, i.e. if there is a danger of recidivism.

(e) Rarely; in 1996 two criminal bans. Legally, there is a wide range of administrative measures (imposition of additional duties ['Anordnungen']; prohibitions ['Untersagungen'], including the closing down of an installation).

(f) Difficult to assess, certainly the 'criminal networks' are difficult to control.

6. Transfrontier pollution incidents

(a) Illegal transboundary transport of waste, illegal transboundary river pollution, illegal export and import of plants and animals of protected species. In some cases specialized police units investigated the illegal export of more then 5,000 tons of hazardous waste. The maximum quantities were to be exported to western European States.

(b) Problems of gathering of evidence; problems of linking the result of the crime to its source and the responsible offenders, esp. if the illegal act was committed by employees of an enterprise; problems of cooperation by way of mutual legal assistance procedures.

Furthermore investigations are difficult when they concern crimes committed over a long period of time.

The big cases are a mixture of environmental and white-collar crime, therefore a twofold training of the investigating officers is mandatory. In some cases different standards of environmental law or different standards of taking and analysing samples caused problems.

(c) At any rate, there is a sufficient number of bodies of international cooperation. This cooperation has to be deepened in intensity, not in organization. Improvements are to be expected (Extension of the application of the Schengen Agreement by the Treaty of Amsterdam; improvements of the instruments on mutual legal assistance on the level of the EU and the Council of Europe). In addition a more efficient fight against environmental crime requires a better training of the police officers, public prosecutors and judges.

7. Criminal liability for environmental offences by public servants and public authorities

(a) Civil servants can be held criminally liable if their administrative authority acts like an enterprise. If civil servants are involved as representatives of the administrative authority as a licensing or supervisory body, criminal liability as a main offender depends on the structure of the offence. In addition, civil servants may be held liable for damages caused by their acts when contributing to the environmental offence. Disciplinary measures and sanctions may be imposed.

(b) N/A

(c) A civil servant,.e.g. the person responsible for an illegal permit, can be the main offender, a co-offender, an assistant to the offender or an instigator.

Proof is difficult, as often the civil servant has a wide discretion in acting. Problems of causation and of guilt may arise, too.

(d) Civil servants/public authorities are becoming more cautious. Tendency to cover themselves, e.g. by calling in superior authorities.

8. Miscellaneous

(a) Administrative measures and sanctions may be effective; the deterrent effect of the possibility to impose imprisonment in serious cases should not be underestimated.

(b) An assessment is difficult as in many cases of minor importance penal fines (for criminal offences) or non-penal fines (for administrative offences) are imposed. In the administrative field this is reflected in the fine catalogues of the states ('Länder'). This does not exclude the alternative use of criminal warnings; discontinuance of criminal proceedings if a certain amount of money is paid to a charity or an environmental organization, or an order of restitution of damages is imposed.

(c) No important role for intelligence services. Police is important but is to a certain extend dependent on information and knowledge of the environmental bodies which might be given only in a hesitant way.

I. Responsible bodies for investigation and prosecution

Responsible bodies for investigation and prosecution are the prosecution authorities ('Staatsanwaltschaften'), the criminal police ('Kriminalpolizei') and specialized bodies of the police, e.g. water protection police ('Wasserschutzpolizei'), as well as the police in general as points of first contact. There are quite a number of police forces. While State police forces do the bulk of the investigation, federal police forces concentrate as a rule on coordinating activities:

- Police stations/headquarters (State authorities): investigation with specialized departments for environmental crimes, sometimes additional tasks e.g. in some States monitoring of waste shipments
- Federal Bureau of Investigation: focal point for national and international investigations concerning environmental crime, intelligence work/exchange of information; co-ordination and support in foreign criminal investigations, own investigations in cases of special interest, development of counteractive measures, membership in INTERPOL Working Parties
- State/Länder Bureaux of Investigation: mainly co-ordinating activities
- Water Police (State authority): investigations on larger rivers and in harbours
- Federal Border Police: investigations at territorial seas and within the Exclusive Economic Zone, investigations on sites owned by the Federal Railway
- Customs (federal authority): monitoring the import and export of goods, including related criminal investigations
- Mining Authorities (State authority): (not as a main task) criminal investigations on mining sites.

II. Name and full address of contact persons

1. Eckard Meyer-Rutz
   Federal Ministery of the Environment, RefL G15
   Alexanderplatz 6, 10178 Berlin
   T ++49–228–305–2252; F ++49–228–305–2225

2. Dr. Möhrenschlager
Federal Ministry of Justice
Heinemannstraße 6, 53170 Bonn
T ++49–228–58–4214; F ++49–228–58–4525
3. Claus-Peter Holz
Federal Bureau of Investigation
65173 Wiesbaden
T ++49–611–55–5738; F ++49–611–55–5753
4. Martin Ittershagen
Federal Environmental Agency, FG I 2.1
Bismarckplatz 1, 14193 Berlin
T++49–30–8903–2124; F ++49–30–8903–2906

III. Brief information on the system of investigation and criminal prosecution of suspected environmental crimes (Structure of national legal prosecution system)

Germany is a federal State in which investigation and prosecution are chiefly done by State (Länder) bodies which are *not* supervised by federal bodies.

The investigations are formally led by the (State) public prosecutor, the (State) police is obliged to support the public prosecutor. Enforcing bodies (with few exceptions: State authorities) can be questioned by the public prosecutor. As a rule enforcing bodies are obliged by internal guidelines to notify suspected crimes to the public prosecutor.

Federal public prosecutors concentrate as a rule on appeal cases, federal police forces chiefly coordinate national and international police activities.

7. ITALY

Respondent: Mr. Mario Scaramella

1. Criminal liability of Corporations for Environmental Offences

(a) No. Unlike other systems of criminal law, which contemplate the possibility of a criminal liability attached to statutorily defined persons, henceforth including corporations, the Italian system only admits criminal liability of physical persons. This is the constant interpretation offered by most Courts and commentators of article 27.1 in combination with article 27.3, Italian Constitution, a principle generally referred to as *societas delinquere non potest*. In cases in which criminal laws refer to the exercise of an economic activity on the part of a juridical person, criminal liability is reconducible to the person(s) acting as the legal representative(s) of the company.

(b) Yes. (owners, governing directors and general managers, and in principle all legal representatives are always liable; other persons can be considered liable only if they have a specific mandate – responsibility for a certain duty).

(c) A distinction must be drawn between environmental crimes that determine consequences of a penal or rather of an administrative nature. In the case of the latter it is in many instances irrelevant the presence of a subjective element: the simple occurrence of a polluting event gives way to the obligation to pay damages and restore pristine state. In all other cases liability must always be proven. Based on the governing principle of the responsibility of the legal representative, the environmental safety obligation rests with the persons identifiable as *ex lege* qualified to act on behalf of the company. In cases provided for by the law, these persons have to prove their '*diligentia*' in having adopted all the prevention measures to avoid the accident, thus assuming the burden of the proof. As to the transfer of the security obligation to other individuals that may have acted on behalf of the company or actually caused the pollution accident, its feasibility is governed by the institute of 'delegation', which is constantly undergoing review and clarification on the part of the jurisprudence. Thus far, and by way of a non exhaustive exemplification, it is possible to say that such delegation must be explicit and freely accepted by a subject who possesses both the necessary technical skills to carry out the tasks provided for and a real decision-making autonomy.

(d) Companies can be condemned to indirect sanctions, such as fiscal and financial fines or the suspensions of activities. Companies can be also condemned to damages.

(e) Companies are usually responsible for the most dangerous and massive environmental offences, thus rendering such inability a significative weakness of the legal system of protection of the environment. Being imposed to physical persons, penalties (for instance a fine) are measured according to the personal properties and not to the Company's ones. It must be noted though that special laws (such as the one on water pollution) provide also special penalties, such as the condemnation to damages, the restoration of the previous environmental conditions and so forth. Finally, being comminuted to physical persons, penalties 'extinguish' with the non imputability of the offender.

2. The role of enforcing bodies and individuals in connection with environmental offences

(a) The trial procedure for environmental offences like for the other criminal offences under Italian law is divided in three consequential moments: 1) acknowledgement of crimes, 2) preliminary investigation about the suspected offences and 3) proper prosecution, including the official investigation and the trial. As far as this latter phase is concerned, the reformed Italian Code of Criminal Procedure (1991) identifies a magistrate, the Public Prosecutor (*Pubblico Ministero*), as the institutional body in charge. All police corps and administrative service with judicial police qualification collaborate with the judiciary for the investigations on environmental crimes (for further details please refer back to the questionnaire submitted for the first WPG in Copenhagen).

(b) The initiative for criminal prosecution rests with the Public Prosecutor, but individuals or recognized associations can inform the public authority of the occurrence of an environmental crime (*notitia criminis*). They can also, as damaged subjects, institute a civil action in the criminal procedure.

(c) Yes, such permission is necessary to commence the prosecution.

(d) They can inform the authority of the occurrence of events that may integrate an offence under criminal law. In a second moment, only recognized associations (ex. environmental associations or public institutions themselves) can intervene in the proceedings (art. 91 penal procedure code) with all the powers and rights typical of the person offended. They can sue for damages in a civil proceeding (art. 74, penal procedure code).

(e) Please refer back to the answers to questions b and d.

(f) Yes, both by helping out the public prosecutor in the gathering of information and by favouring his or her confrontation with the positions of civil society in these that can be at times highly sensitive topics.

(g) The public prosecutor, according to Italian Criminal Procedure Code, is in charge of the direction of the investigation, the judicial police and all police corps and administrative services with judicial police qualification have the task to support him or her in the official investigation, and are obviously in charge of verifying the *notitia criminis* in the unofficial investigation that precedes. Amongst the environmental police corps we find: Polizia di Stato, which depends on the Minister of Interior, does not dispose of specific environmental offices but sometimes works on nature conservation if related to serious organized crime or if related to public security issue or health safety. Carabinieri, that depend on the Ministry of defence, dispose of an operational ecological unit (Nucleo Ecologico Operativo – NOE). The Guardia di Finanza, which depends on the Ministry of Finance, has worked in hundreds of environmental investigations related to their mandate in fiscal and financial matters, and are now in the process of developing a new role as environmental police experts. The Corpo Forestale dello Stato, depending on the Ministry of Agriculture and Forests, has assumed the role of environmental police with special expertise in fauna and flora protection and protection of national parks (more on this in the report on the first WPG).

(h) The lack of a sufficient degree of public awareness on environmental issues in Italy results in a weak contribution of both enforcing bodies and civil society to a proper enforcement of environmental law.

3. Criminal penalties

(a) There is a double system of sanctions: penal and administrative. The administrative ones consist in the payment of a fine that is proportioned to the gravity of the offence; penal sanctions are imposed only for environmental crimes and consist in the arrest and in the payment of a certain amount of money. There is also another kind of sanctions, 'the complementary sanctions' such as the suspension of the activity. For all kind of offences (including crimes) the law provides for the obligation to pay for the environmental damage and the obligation to the restoration of the previous environmental situation (I. 349/86)

(b) Administrative sanctions are those that found application most often. By way of an example as to their nature and entity we can cite the following:
   - Water pollution: opening of new water waste pipe without authorization: prison from 2 months to 2 years either alone or with a fine from approximately 300 ECU to 5,000 ECU. Offences in protected areas: prison up to 12 months and fine from approx. 110 ECU to 22,000 ECU. For further details on this topic, please refer back to our annex to the first Impel questionnaire in occasion of the working group in Copenhagen.

(c) Imprisonment and fines of substantial amounts.

(d) The discrimination in the application of the typology of sanctions is once again due to the weak public awareness as to the importance of a proper enforcement of the norms protecting the environment, as well as to the strength of the economic interests affected. In this perspective it is readily understandable how administrative sanctions of a limited entity are more easily comminuted, also in consideration of the more informal judicial iter that brings to their imposition.

(e) Always and necessarily by the court or by the monocratic judicial authority (*Pretore*). In special circumstances, expressly provided for by the law, an injunction (*decreto esecutivo*) can be ordered by the public prosecutor (who is himself a magistrate). It should be noted that such an injunction, although carrying executive consequences, is not a criminal sanction.

4. Administrative Sanctions

(a) Yes, administrative bodies can impose fines without any criminal proceeding.

(b) No. they are administrative in the legislative definition of the illicit event, as well as in the nature of the judicial proceeding and the authoritative body to whose competence they are submitted.

(c) The Italian law system, as already noted, does have two types of sanction of environmental offences. The first type, administrative or contraventional sanction, is generally comminuted for less serious offences; usually it is more immediate and damages the wealth of the offender. The second, carrying penal consequences, is provided of in the case of heavy offences. It can only be comminuted as the result of the completion of a full criminal proceeding and therefore requires much more time and formal complexity. Needless to say, given the disparity of the consequences for the offender, the relationship of criminal to administrative sanctions is one of major to minor, both in scale and deterrent effect.

(d) Such fines are not frequently imposed, although more often than criminal ones.

(e) It does not contribute to the significant extent that we all would hope for, because administrative fines are seldom concretely imposed, due to lack of controls in environmental law enforcement.

5. Existence of Instruments which Prohibit individuals from carrying out a similar activity

(a) Yes. The entire system of Italian environmental legislation is based on the principle of responsibility towards the environment in the carrying out of an economic or other activity. Henceforth, several examples can be found of such provisions, invalidating licences or otherwise banning the continued exercise of a profession or of an activity in cases of environmental offences.

(b) It can be both an administrative sanction and an accessory sanction to a criminal sentence.

(c) The notice or other provision in case can be served by the Court, by the public prosecutor or by the competent administrative authority, depending on the nature of the offence and therefore of the sanction, as specified under c.

(d) As already said, such notices are accessory sanctions of widespread provision and application. By way of an absolutely not exhaustive example, we can cite the suspension of the fishing licence and the interdiction from the exercise of maritime fishing comminuted to those who violate the normative on the protection of biological resources and maritime fishing.

(e) Very frequently employed.

(f) Although often used, these instruments do not always achieve satisfactory levels of effectiveness, mainly due, as correctly suggested in the question to the difficulty of tracking back the effective owner or referent of an economic activity.

6. Transfrontier pollution incidents

(a) The Prosecutor office of Reggio Calabria, in agreement with other seven district prosecutors, investigated on the hypothesis of the sinking of about 80 ships, containing radioactive waste coming from different countries, in Italian and international waters. The person suspected is the Italian manager of a Swiss firm involved in army traffic and radioactive waste disposal at sea. The ships were identified on the bottom of the sea in different areas (up to the depth of 2,500 meters and the distance of 30 miles from the coasts) and the criminal evidence about the nuclear traffic was obtained by a strong co-operation with judicial police (Carabinieri), secret serves (SISMI and SISDE) and international consultants (Special Research Monitoring Centre experts).

(b) In our experience, the main problems faces are concerned with very little or no assistance offered in support of the investigating and prosecuting magistrate, no enforcement on the part of Interpol and customs police authority, a lack of exercise of jurisdiction on the part of European Union organisms and institutions and, above all, an almost complete absence of collaboration in the exchange of confidential information at the international level.

(c) Most definitely not. In the case described sub a), to bring one clear example, the captain and the shipowner of one of the sunk ships object of the investigation, both Greek citizens, took refuge in the territory of that State and did not make themselves available for collaboration with the investigation. No support was offered on the part of Greek authorities.

7. Criminal liability for environmental offences by public servants and public authorities

(a) Yes, civil servants and public authorities are capable of being held criminally liable for environmental offences.

(b) —

(c) Besides criminal responsibility, civil servants have accounting responsibility for damages to the State.

(d) Not in a way that would be auspicable, due to the scarcity of control of the law.

8. Miscellaneous

(a) The administrative sanctions would in principle be more effective because of their direct application and because they damage the wealth of transgressor. Unfortunately, this effectiveness suffers for reasons exposed sub 4.e and 5.f.

(b) A tolerance of minor breaches is definitely to be found sometimes due to the perceived impossibility to intervene in a very strict manner on a highly difficult and deteriorated territorial situation, sometimes with a more or less official collusion of public authorities.

(c) No.

(d) About the monitoring knowledge of crimes, the police often receives inputs to open a preliminary investigation by the intelligence services. The two main offices of intelligence for security and information are SISDE of the Ministry of Interiors and SISMI of the Minister of Defence. A call was recently directed to them by the President of the Government for a special effort in the new challenge of national and international security: environmental security issues, to testify of a new role for them in this field.

Brief Information on the system of investigation and criminal prosecution of suspected environmental crimes (Structure of the national legal prosecution system)

Investigation Prosecution

Within the penal jurisdiction sphere, it is possible to identify different consequential moments of prosecution (latu sensu):

1) the acknowledgement of crimes;
2) the first investigation about a suspected offence;
3) the official investigation able to produce evidence for the judiciary and
4) the preliminary judgement. Following procedures regard the different levels of trial.

The new Italian criminal procedures code (1991) identifies in the role of the Public Prosecutor (a magistrate), the direction of the investigation, leaving to judicial police only the proceedings sub points 1 and 2 above mentioned (with the duty to inform the judiciary in 48 hours after the acquisition of the 'notitia criminis' and the task to support the Prosecutor in the following actions.

All the police corps and administrative services with 'judicial police' qualification are in charge for the investigation about environmental crimes. Few cases of cooperation between the corps, in environmental matters, are acknowledged. The most important police corps are the state police (Polizia di Stato), the military police (Carabinieri), the revenue military police (Guardia di Finanza), the foresters (Corpo Forestale dello Stato). These corps are legitimized by the 1991 Penal Procedure Code (artt. 55 and ss.) and by the Law n. 349.86 (institution of the Ministry of the Environment) to work as environmental police and to organize special units in charge for environmental issues.

The 'Polizia di Stato' (100,000 agents), which depends on the Minister of Interior, does not dispose of specific environmental offices but sometimes works on nature conservation if related to serious organized crime activities (for instance the confiscation of hundreds of billions of Italian lire was done in 1991 against Mafia patrimony in application of environmental laws) or if related to public security issues or health safety.

The 'Carabinieri' (112,000 agents), Ministry of Defence, dispose of an operational ecological unit (Nucleo Operativo Ecologico – NOE), the oldest in Europe together with the Spanish Gendarmeria ecological group, which is formed at present by 140 elements depending on the Minister of the Environment and which are related to the territorial structure of the corp (hundreds of offices, stations and special groups). In the last three years the NOE made 80,000 controls identifying 43,000 offences and 47,000 offenders (47 of which were arrested); real estates for 35 millions of ECU were sequestrated during 1,500 operations. The development of this body is confirmed by a special section involved in radioactive waste investigation and by the recent institution of NOE offices in each town. The new waste law (the so-called 'Decreto Ronchi' includes provisions (art. 20 cm. 5) which give to the NOE special and 'typified' functions of environmental police. It is then possible to identify the 'Carabinieri' as the main environmental investigation service.

The 'Guardia di Finanza' (66,000 agents), which depends on the Minister of Finance, worked in hundreds of environmental investigations, sometimes related to fiscal, treasury of financial inquires, and has created specialized units care of their naval and air services. The Corp has recently requested to the University of Naples the high qualification in environmental police strategies of the Commanders in charge for the different judicial, naval and air services, so that they will be able on their turn to form their subordinates: in a few months also the revenue service will be in charge as an expert environmental police corp.

The 'Corpo Forestale dello Stato', Ministry of Agriculture and Forests, is the corp in charge for forest police at national level. After the institution of the Ministry of the Environment it changed tasks and aims, developing the role of environmental police with special expertise in fire investigations, fauna and flora protection (CITES Convention application included), protection of National Parks and much more.

A new National Environmental Agency (ANPA) and some regional agencies (ARPA) are in charge as environmental authorities and their role include functions of judicial and administrative police with special power and typified functions. In the next future these administrations will represent the operational instruments for 'full' investigations in environmental matters considering the availability in legislative enforcement and scientific analytical employment.

Other judicial police services involved at national or local level in environmental investigations are:

- the coast-guard, maritime authority in charge as coastal environmental police
- the zoophilous guards (Law 611.1913), which depends on the Society for the protection of animals and other voluntary guards which depends by environmental associations if authorized by the Ministry of the Interior
- the officers of the Ministry of Industries (Law RDL 2033.1925);
- guards authorized for the surveillance of public and private waters (Law RD 1604.1931)
- health officers (Law RDL 1265.1934)
- commanders of local and departmental bodies of the Armed Forces (art. 301 c.p.m.p.)
- fire brigade officers of the Ministry of Interior
- postal inspectors of the Ministry of Telecommunications (Law DPR 156.1973; DM 14.8.1943)
- fishing inspectors (Law DPR 747.1954)
- mine corp inspectors and engineers (Law DPR 128.1959)
- agriculture frauds inspectors (Law 1304.1961)
- custom services (DPR 43.1973)
- public works ministry officers (Law 64.1974)
- hunt officers (Law 157.92)
- national mineral office (Law 886.1979)
- municipal corps and guards (Law 65.1986)
- provincial services and guards (Law 133.1992)

(...)

DENOUNCER PARTIES

Citizens, private-law associations, grass roots movements, political parties, local and national administrations are typical denouncer and informer subjects which give to the criminal prosecution machine the starting input. A brief analysis conducted at

local level confirms that the main part of the investigations developed by the authorities above mentioned starts by local authorities and non-governmental organizations. Procedures initiated by municipalities are the most relevant part in statistics but sometimes they regard cases not well reported by media or not discussed at all (cases which seem not interesting for the community); cases reported by important NCO's and political parties (in Italy strictly related) are generally show-effects notices of illicit cases which obtain attention by the media and by the judiciary. It is necessary to underline the lack of participation in the judgement of NCO's and local authorities, for instance as civil parts or victims of environmental crimes (after the first years the special fund of the Environmental Ministry for legal expenses of the NCO involved in judgements was abolished because no money had been used!).
Police and administrative authorities (ministries, regions, provinces, municipalities, national parks, agencies and others) must inform as soon as possible the Judicial Public Prosecutor about suspected environmental crimes. The judge, when it is possible, confirms the police in the investigation under his control and provides for the acquisition of all the criminal evidences that will be discussed in front of a Preliminary Judgement Court and, if necessary, in front of the different jurisdiction.

PROSECUTORS AND COURTS

Environmental prosecutions at judicial level can involve different types of courts:

- An offence against water, soil, air, wildlife or natural beauties generally involves the 'single' judgement of the 'Pretore', a judge which can punish with penalties up to four years of prison and related fines (as sanctioned in the penal code for the different hypothesis); almost every municipality has a 'Pretore' which is part of a 'Pretura Circondariale', a provincial office which includes a Public Prosecution body (sometimes these prosecution offices have a specialized section working on environmental matters).
- Environmental crimes involving organized criminality or public officers and other serious illicit actions related to nature conservation are under the jurisdiction of a Tribunal which can punish the offender with sanctions up to 24 years of prison and related fines (as indicated in the penal code). Each province or 'important' town has a Tribunal which includes a Public Prosecutor office.
- Crimes punished by the law with imprisonment up to life sentence and related sanctions (for instance genocide related with environmental crimes) are a competence of special Courts 'de Assize ed Appello' which are present in the main town. A General Public Prosecutor Office, in charge for the prosecutions 'in Assise' and for the appeal judgements, is located by these Courts and is in charge for the coordination of the other prosecutors in the district.

Final appeals are possible by the 'Corte Suprema di Cassazione', located in the capital city, whose sentences are the most important under the legislative interpretation profiles and jurisprudence. A General Prosecutor by the Supreme court is the national coordinator of Public Prosecutors offices and policies.

No administrative courts in charge for criminal jurisdiction exist in environmental matters (they exist for example for juvenile delinquency). There are some Courts which are able to punish with administrative sanctions some illicit cases identified by rules or administrative laws, for instance in water matters (Tribunale delle Acque).

COOPERATION BETWEEN ADMINISTRATIVE AND JUDICIAL BODIES

Cooperation between administrative bodies and judiciary often represents an important instrument for the application of the environmental law: some legal provisions enable the magistrates (including the prosecutors) to nominate individual consultants or to use adviser services of administrations. Cooperation between these administrations and the police is also possible and it is often used by the officers to support the enforcer with analysts and environmental experts.

If the advice is requested by the Prosecutor, this part of the investigation can only be used in the contradictory (judgements must be given after full agreement by both sides); if it is requested by the Court or by the Police in the immediateness of the crime (before the activation of the Prosecutor) it represents an evidence which can be used directly by the judge.

Prosecutors and Judges, in any moment of the prosecution, can request the administrations the production of relevant documents for the proceedings.

8. THE NETHERLANDS

Respondent: Ms. M.H. de Weert

1. Criminal liability of Corporations for Environmental Offences

(a) Yes.

(b) Yes.

(c) The court has to decide whether the company can be held responsible for the criminal behaviour of one or more employees. It is not necessary to prove liability against an individual employee as long as it is clear that the company could decide whether the – for instance – pollution incident happened or not and, as long as it is clear that the company accepts or normally accepts this kind of behaviour of the employees.

A company, the persons who lead the company and also the employees can generally be held criminally liable for environmental and other offences. All of them – apart of together – can be prosecuted.

(d) —

(e) —

2. The role of enforcing bodies and individuals in connection with environmental offences

(a) The public prosecutor.

(b) No.

(c) See under a.

(d) —

(e) An individual can complain in court about the decision of a public prosecutor not to prosecute someone on the condition that the individual has a direct interest in the case; an individual can also engage in a criminal procedure and ask for compensation.

(f) —

(g) The public prosecutor is the leader of the investigation; the police has the most important role in the investigation of environmental offences – many enforcement bodies support the police in their investigations.

(h) The administrative enforcing bodies certainly contribute to a proper enforcement of environmental law. They have enough instruments to a proper enforcement. The only problem is that the administrative enforcement bodies seem to wait very long before taking administrative measures towards the offender.

The criminal enforcing bodies also contribute to a proper enforcement of environmental law. They also have enough enforcement instruments.

Individuals can charge a person or a company and provoke an investigation by the police.

3. Criminal penalties

(a) Sanctions:

- fine
- imprisonment
- dismissal of certain rights
- shut down of the company
- confiscation
- publication of the judgement
- absorption of a legal gain
- victim compensation
- conviction to carry out what has been left undone
- conviction to restore the harm

(b) Fines

Examples:

- small company without licence: from 450 EUR.
- small water pollution: from 650 EUR.
- put fertilizer on the soil without avoiding emission of minerals etc.: 1.100 EUR.

In severe cases very high fines are applied, for instance several hundred thousands of euro's. In severe cases against persons imprisonment is applied.

(c) All sanctions except the fine and the imprisonment.

(d) The other sanctions are sanctions with heavy consequences for the defendant; to execute these sanctions the public prosecutor often needs the cooperation of the administrative bodies. Sometimes the administrative authority has applied an administrative sanction which has the same consequences for the defendant as the criminal sanction.

(e) By the public prosecutor and the court.

4. Administrative Sanctions

(a) No.
There is a discussion going on in the Netherlands about the question whether administrative bodies should be able to impose fines.

(b) —

(c) The various kinds of sanctions can be imposed apart from each other. It is important, however, to coordinate the imposture of the sanctions.

- Administrative sanctions: are imposed only to influence future behaviour;
- Criminal sanctions: are also imposed to punish actual offences.
- The effects of the administrative and criminal sanctions are comparable.

(d) —

(e) —

5. Existence of Instruments which Prohibit individuals from carrying out a similar activity

(a) Yes, the sanction of dismissal of certain rights.

(b) A criminal sanction.

(c) By the court.

(d) This instrument is hardly practised in the Netherlands. It should only be imposed in severe cases, when offences have been committed by companies. The main reason why this instrument is hardly practised is that imposing this sanction is not very useful in most cases, because the place of the condemned person (in the company) can simply be taken over by someone else.

(e) Rarely

(f) See under d.

6. Transfrontier pollution incidents

(a) We had two main investigations of import of household waste. Dutch defendants imported the waste out of Germany and exported the waste to countries in the 'third world' without fulfilling the obligations of the European Regulation nr. 259/93.

(b) It takes time to get the necessary information from the authorities of other states.

Sometimes you don't get all the information you asked for.
Sometimes the policy in another country sees the alleged offences in a different way, which influences the attitude of the authorities towards these offences.

In general, the cooperation between the neighbouring countries is good.

(c) Yes.

7. Criminal liability for environmental offences by public servants and public authorities

(a) Yes, unless they catty out a specific government task. A long time it has not been clear whether a public authority could be held criminally liable for environment offences. Now it is clear, thanks to a recent judgement of the High Court (Hoge Raad -Pikmeer II-arrest).

(b) —

(c) The system works the same when prosecuting an individual or a public authority.

(d) I think so, because a penal case before court has a great impact. The criminal liability is very important, because in some cases the democratic control of the public authority doesn't find place at all.

8. Miscellaneous

(a) In general administrative sanctions are very effective. The problem is, however, that the public authorities are not very eager no imposing administrative sanctions.

(b) The public prosecution office has the policy to use a small tolerance of minor breaches.

Public authorities: the government of the Netherlands has the policy to minimalize tolerance by public authorities. (That discussion concerns greater breaches).

Public authorities however like to enforce by seeking an agreement between authority and individual, they always see individuals and companies as trustworthy.

(c) In the Netherlands the intelligence services have an important role in environmental investigations. They work together with the police. In environmental cases the role of the intelligence service is different from its role in other investigations. In environmental cases there is less secret information than in other cases. Mostly, the information supplied by the intelligence service can be used in criminal proceedings.

9. PORTUGAL

Respondent: Mr. Padro Portugal

1. Criminal liability of Corporations for Environmental Offences

(a) By the articles 11° and 12° of the new Penal Code (Decree Law n° 48/95, of March 15th), the general rule impose the criminal liability for the singular persons.

(b) It is possible lawsuiting the directors or managers of a company.

(c) Yes, it is necessary proved the liability against an individual employed who has caused the pollution incident.

(d) The answer in a was yes, so this question is damaged.

2. The role of enforcing bodies and individuals in connection with environmental offences

(a) The general rule impose the competence at the public prosecution.

(b) Yes, the individuals and also the environmental protection associations have competence for bring criminal prosecutions for environmental offences.

(c) Yes.

(d) The individuals stay assistances of the process. The advantage consist in the autonomy accusation for himself.

(e) The answer in b was yes, so this question is damaged.

(f) No. We have at moment a satisfactory coordination between these bodies and the public prosecutor.

(g) The enforcing bodies for example, police authorities or administrative authorities, have an important role in the investigation, because is with this authorities the process are started.

(h) Enlargement procedure legitimate for this bodies.

3. Criminal penalties

(a) The penalties stipulated in criminal law consist of custodial sentences commutable in fines.

(b) The criminal fines.

(c) The custodial sentences.

(d) Only since October 1st 1995 we have the new Penal Code where are stipulated two environmental crimes, one of these concerns the protection of nature (article 278), and the other refers to pollution (article 279), so there is still no relevant legal history in this area.

(e) Only for the Common Courts.

4. Administrative Sanctions

(a) Yes, they have this possibility.

(b) This fines are purely administrative sanction.

(c) The relationship between civil or administrative sanctions with the criminal sanctions consist in total independence of procedure.

(d) The fines imposed by the administrative authorities are very frequently is the procedure more efficient.

(e) I think this kind of procedure have a good contribute for enforcement the environmental law in Portugal.

5. Existence of Instruments which Prohibit individuals from carrying out a similar activity

(a) Yes, we have complementary penalties for the transgressor's. For example the transgressor's belongings being seized, the transgressor's subsidies being retained and also their license to operate being suspended for up to two years.

(b) This complementary penalties are applicated by administrative bodies.

(c) This notice also served in the Court, or by the public prosecutor.

(d) When we speak in administrative sanctions it is the same and also commonly known by Administrative Penal Law, so the investigation and sentencing decision are carried out by the administrative authorities with the courts only becoming involved at the appeal stage.

(e) The application of the instruments at Administrative Penal Law are very frequently.

(f) Yes it is possible.

6. Transfrontier pollution incidents

(a) We don't have many problems with transfrontier pollution.

(b) The particular problems are in water of the rivers between Portugal and Spain.

(c) Yes.

7. Criminal liability for environmental offences by public servants and public authorities

(a) The singular's persons and the titles of public authorities can be criminally liable for environmental offences.

(b) The answer in a was yes, so this question is damaged.

(c) It is the common system.

(d) No.

8. Miscellaneous

(a) Yes.

(b) The administrative sanctions are more efficacious then penal sanctions.

(c) No.

(d) Yes, we have a satisfactory coordination and cooperation between this bodies.

10. SPAIN

Respondent: Mr. Angeles Naves

1. Criminal liability of Corporations for Environmental Offences

(a) No. Corporations do not have criminal liability. They have liability of an administrative nature and subsidiary civil liability.

(b) Whoever acts as administrator, whether de facto or by right, of a corporate entity or in the name or legal or voluntary representation of another, shall be personally liable, even if he does not meet the conditions, qualities or relations that the corresponding figure of crime of offences requires for being an active subject of it, if such circumstances occur in the entity or body whose name or representation he holds, Article 31 of the Criminal Code. It is therefore the executives of companies who are criminally liable for environmental offences committed by the companies they administrate or represent.

(c) It is necessary to prove the liability individually, either against whoever has expressly caused it or against the executives or heads of those companies.

(d) The answer in section a.

(e) Application of the Criminal Code.

2. The role of enforcing bodies and individuals in connection with environmental offences

(a) Criminal Court, Provincial Court and, in appeals, the Supreme Court.

(b) When directly aggrieved by means of private accusation, if not, only by means of people's action.

(c) If there is no people's action, the attorney's permission is needed.

(d) The proceedings commence before the Criminal Court or before the Provincial Court and, in appeals, before the Supreme Court.

(e) —

(f) No.

(g) Very important since they are parties in the criminal trial.

(h) Very positive.

3. Criminal penalties

(a) The committing of crimes against natural resources and the environment, the Criminal Code in Article 325 establishes that:

'Penalties of six months to four years prison, fines of eight to twenty-four months and special disqualification for profession or post for a period of one to three years shall be imposed on those who, contravening the Laws or other provisions of a general character that protect the environment, directly or indirectly provoke or cause emissions, spillages, radiations, extractions or excavations, dumping, noises, vibrations, injections or deposits into the atmosphere, the soil, the subsoil, or terrestrial, marine or underground waters, having consequences, including in transfrontier spaces, as well as the drawing of water that might seriously harm the balance of natural systems. If the risk of serious damage concerns the health of people, the penalty of prison shall be imposed in its the upper half.'

Article 326 in turn establishes that:

'The penalty that is higher in degree shall be imposed, without prejudice to that which might correspond pursuant to the stipulations of this Code when, in the committing of whatsoever of the events described in article 325, any of the following circumstances occur:

That the industry or activity is functioning clandestinely, without the required authorization or administrative approval of its installations having been obtained.

That express orders from the administrative authority to correct or suspend the activities listed in the above article have been disobeyed.

That information regarding the environmental aspects of the same have been falsified or concealed.

That the inspection activity of the Administration has been obstructed.

That a risk has occurred of irreversible or catastrophic deterioration.

That an illegal extraction of water has been made during a period of drought.'

In all cases provided for in the above two articles, the Judge of Tribunal shall be able to agree to the closing of the company, its premises or establishments, temporarily or permanently. Temporary closure may not exceed five years (Article 129).

(b) The application of fines is much more common than the application of prison penalties.

(c) There is no knowledge of what type of sanction is rarely applied, though the offence that is most rarely sanctioned is indeed known, which is forest fires.

(d) Data gathered from the Annual Report of the Attorney's Office of the Madrid Higher Court of Justice.

(e) The Spanish Constitution only grants this authority to Judges and Tribunals.

4. Administrative Sanctions

(a) Yes.

(b) Yes.

(c) In our Legal Code, there exist administrative, civil and criminal sanctions. If there is a criminal sanction, there cannot be an administrative one, but a criminal sanction can have a civil sanction implicitly associated with it. The three types of penalty are not equivalent since administrative sanctions are assessed in economic terms and criminal ones implicitly involve the loss of freedom or of rights.

(d) This depends on the number of inspections made.

(e) Yes, without any doubt.

5. Existence of Instruments which Prohibit individuals from carrying out a similar activity

(a) Yes. There are provisional measures.

(b) This is an administrative tool regulated in art. 136 of the Law of Juridical Systems and Common Administrative Procedure: 'When so provided in the rules governing the sanctioning procedures, it shall be possible to proceed by means of a reasoned agreement to adopt measures of a provisional nature that ensure the efficacy of the final decision that might apply.'

(c) Yes.

(d) The Law of Juridical Systems and Common Administrative Procedure establishes that once the procedure has been initiated, the competent administrative body for deciding on it shall be able to adopt the provisional measures that it considers appropriate for ensuring the efficacy of the decision, but provisional measures may not be issued that imply a violation of rights provided for by the laws (art. 72).

(e) It is frequent.

(f) It is a preventive measure.

6. Transfrontier pollution incidents

(a) None known so far. No case has occurred of transfrontier incidents that have led to a judicial trial.

(b) Not known.

(c) No.

7. Criminal liability for environmental offences by public servants and public authorities

(a) Yes.

(b) —

(c) Regulated in the Criminal Code, an offence committed by a public servant is punished with greater severity when these crimes are committed against the environmental and natural resources. Prevarication, i.e. the action of a public servant who, knowing that it is unjust, issues an arbitrary decision in an administrative matter, is punished with the penalty of special disqualification for employment or public post for a period of seven to ten years (art. 404).

Nevertheless, this crime of prevarication is aggravated when it comes to actions against the environment. In this case, a public servant who knowingly issues a favourable report on construction projects or the granting of licences contrary to the urban development regulations shall, in addition tot the penalty of article 404, be punished with between six months and two years prison or a fine of twelve to twenty-four months (art. 320). If the public servant or authority knowingly issues a favourable report on the granting of manifestly illegal licences authorising the functioning of pollutant industries or activities, or which on the occasion of their inspections conceals an infringement of the laws or of the regulating provisions of a general nature governing them, the term of prison shall be from six months to three years or a fine of eight to twenty-four months (art. 329).

(d) Answered in the above section.

8. Miscellaneous

(a) Not too much.

(b) An administrative sanction or procedure is imposed in line with the degree of the breach, but also in line with the environmental damage caused.

(c) There exists good collaboration. The information supplied by these services can be used as proof in a criminal proceeding.

11. SWEDEN

Respondent: Ms. Viktoria Ljung
Brief Information on the system of investigation and criminal prosecution of suspected environmental crimes (Structure of the national legal prosecution system)

The public prosecutor

The public prosecutor is a link in the important chain of official bodies – police, public prosecutor, court of law and correctional service – which shall protect the community against crime. The public prosecutor holds a central position in criminal proceedings. His chief duties are

- to direct investigations of crime
- to make decisions in prosecution issues
- to prosecute in court

Conduct of preliminary investigation

When a crime has come to the knowledge of the police an investigation is initiated. The public prosecutor enters into the picture as supervisor of the investigation when it has reached the stage at which, as it is said, someone may reasonably be suspected of the crime. In cases of a less serious nature, however, the police generally conduct investigations to their completion.

However, as to environmental offences a report is made directly to the public prosecutor, who then takes charge of the investigation at an early stage.

The public prosecutor acts in close cooperation with the police. The work as officer in charge of the investigation normally implies that the public prosecutor plans the investigation of a crime in cooperation with the police, directs the way the investigation is to be organized, remains informed about its progress and gives instructions for its continuation.

The public prosecutor shall ensure that a preliminary investigation is conducted efficiently and quickly. At the same time it shall be conducted in a considerate manner and in such a way that circumstances favourable to the suspect also emerge.

The prosecutor's duties during the preliminary investigation also include decisions on questions relating to arrest orders, travel prohibitions, house searches and other coercive measures. If there is reason to deprive the suspect of his/her liberty beyond the period of provisional custody, the prosecutor has to request the court to order that the person under arrest be placed in detention.

Examination of grounds for prosecution

The public prosecutor may decide not to initiate a preliminary investigation or to discontinue if he considers that there are insufficient grounds for its completion. If a preliminary investigation has been completed, the prosecutor must decide on the question of prosecution.

In the first place the public prosecutor must determine whether a crime has been committed and then whether there is sufficient evidence against the suspect. If both questions are answered in the affirmative, the prosecutor must in principle institute prosecution as in Sweden prosecution is obligatory unless otherwise prescribed.

The prosecution is instituted in the district court. But sometimes, by virtue of certain rules of law, the prosecutor may decide not to prosecute. This is known as waives of prosecution. The prosecutor often waives prosecution, above all, of juveniles aged 15–17 years. Generally it is then a matter for the social authorities to decide what measures may be required. Waiver of prosecution also sometimes occurs on grounds of judicial economy, for instance when a person has been sentenced for a crime and new crimes are discovered which are of no major significance from the point of view of sanctions.

In the case of minor offences the prosecutor usually issues an order of summary punishment by fine. If the suspect accepts the order, the case need not be taken to court. It can be said that the prosecutor functions as a judge.

If the prosecutor decides to prosecute, he shall deliver an application for summons to the court. In it he describes the offence or offences of which the defendant is suspected and the evidence against him. Through this description of the crime the prosecutor sets the framework for the coming trial.

As is already apparent, not all decisions lead to prosecution. In recent years the prosecutors have examined the grounds for prosecution of more than 270,000 people each year. Of these about 75,000 have been prosecuted. About 15,000 have been granted a waiver of prosecution, about 8,000 of whom were juvenile offenders. Orders of summary punishment by fine have been issued against more than 75,000 people. In about 100,000 cases the prosecutor has decided not to prosecute for different reasons, principally because of insufficient evidence but also because the act has not proved to be a crime or because the suspect was innocent.

Pleading and appearing in court

Another important part of the public prosecutor's work is the preparation of pleading and appearing in court. Most prosecutors spend one or two days a week in court. In may cases there is a complainant, i.e. a person who has suffered injury from the crime and may therefore have a claim for compensation or damage from the suspect. In criminal proceedings the injured party's claim is often brought by a public prosecutor.

When the district court has pronounced judgement, the prosecutor must decide whether to challenge it and thus take the case on to the Court of Appeal. The judgement of the Court of Appeal can be challenged in the Supreme Court. In such cases the Prosecutor-General institutes the prosecution. Appeal to the Supreme Court at the initiative of the Prosecutor-General occurs in about 20 cases a year.

Organization of the public prosecution system

The country is divided into seven public prosecutor districts (åklagarmyndigheter). One of these districtis is specialized in economic crimes. The head of each public district prosecution is a Director. He directs and supervizes public prosecution in his region of jurisdiction and shall especially take measures to ensure that the regulations governing means of coercion, waiver of prosecution, examination of grounds for prosecution and summary punishment by fine are correctly and uniformly applied. He can review and take over cases dealt with by a local public prosecutor.

The public prosecution districts are organized into local prosecution offices. The 42 local public prosecution offices are each headed by a Chief Prosecutor.

There is also a Public Prosecution Office for Special Cases, including an economic crime unit, headed by a Director. The special prosecutors at this office undertake advanced public prosecuting duties, in particular the prosecution of economic crime in the entire country.

The Prosecutor-General

The Prosecutor-General is, after the Government, the highest public prosecution authority in the country and has responsibility for and the direction of the public prosecution system. He is public prosecutor in the Supreme Court, generally represented by one of the assistant prosecutors to the Prosecutor-General.

The Prosecutor-General can review the decisions of subordinate prosecutors and take over their duties. The Prosecutor-General is also the national administrative authority for the public prosecution system.

Other duties of the Prosecutor-General are to give the public prosecutors advice, information and directions concerning the exercise of their duties and to inspect subordinate authorities. He follows the application of the laws and continuously publishes reports of new cases.

The Prosecutor-General is called upon to a considerable extent as consultative authority in legislative questions.

Staff

About 1,200 are employed at the country's public prosecution offices.
Two third of the employees are prosecutors. Most of the others are clerks engaged in the keeping of journals and records.

Vocational training

The following educational requirements apply to those seeking entry into the public prosecution service as prosecutor candidates.

1. Completion of upper secondary school
2. University law degree (juris kandidatexamen) (an approximately five-year course of study)

3. Law clerk competence, generally acquired through work at a district court for two years.

The prosecutor candidate is employed on a probationary basis at one of the prosecution offices for about nine months. During that time, the candidate is assigned responsibility for carrying out prosecutional tasks in order to familiarize himself with the practical workings of the prosecutorial function.

If the candidate is found suitable for continued employment he will be appointed assistant prosecutor. Following this, he will take part in a two-month course for prosecutors arranged by the office of the Prosecutor-General.

Assistant prosecutors who have been employed for about three years take part in a course of continued training. The course deals mainly with questions related to the handling of specialized cases. Once the assistant prosecutor has completed three years of employment, he receives the title of local public prosecutor.

Swedish environmental Code

Since the first Swedish answers for the report have been given there have been major changes in Swedish environmental legislation. On 1 January 1999, the Environmental Code entered into force, bringing together 15 existing central environmental laws. The reform has also led to the setting up of a new organization for fighting environmental crime.

The overall purpose of the Environmental Code is to promote sustainable development, which will assure a healthy and sound environment for present and future generations. In order to achieve this goal all links in the chain of the Code must work efficiently (i.e. objectives, basic obligations, permits, inspection, reconsideration and penalty for infringement). It is up to the legal system to make sure that the last link in the chain, penalty, really is a realistic final resort when all other ways of protecting the environment has failed. It is equally important that the risk of legal repercussion should be so much of a deterrent that infringement never takes place.

In 1998 the Office of the Prosecutor-General was assigned to draw up a general proposal for procedures for investigating all types of crime against the environment. This included which authorities to be responsible for investigations, co-ordination, competence building, and collaboration between crime-investigation authorities and inspection authorities as well as international work within the field.

The report of the Prosecutor-General includes observations of the current situation that shows that number of environmental crimes reported in Sweden number about 350 a year. With the new legislation and improved collaboration between inspection authorities and crime investigations authorities this number was expected to increase by around 50%. However the amount of incoming cases has largely exceeded the expected number. Last year, 2002, more than 3000 cases were reported to the Prosecutors office. According to a special provision in the Environmental Code, the inspection authorities are obliged to report suspected infringements to the police or to the public prosecute.

Another thing noticed in the report is the problem that representatives of the crime investigation authorities and inspection authorities do not speak 'speak the same language', something often leads to unnecessary misunderstandings. A conclusion is therefor that the authorities must co-operate closely, and that this cooperation must take place at operative level and must include joint training.

Environmental cases are handled by a limited number of public prosecutors and policemen with a special competence. The resources set aside by the Government for fighting environmental crime should be remarked for activities of this nature.

At central level, a special unit for environmental crime fighting has been set up at the Office of the Prosecutor-General. The task of this unit will be co-ordination at national level including contracts with other central authorities, control and follow-up, intelligence work, training, international work etc.

The new organization for fighting environmental crime started operation on 1 January 2000.

12. UNITED KINGDOM

Respondent: Ms. Bridget Marshall

1. Criminal liability of Corporations for Environmental Offences

(a) Yes.

(b) Liability can be both against the company and also directors and/or managers. Principles of vicarious liability apply to bind company. Vicarious liability is a legal principle which ensures that a company is legally bound by the acts of its employees provided they are acting within the ordinary course of their employment.

(c) Principle of what is known as, 'vicarious liability' exists to bind a company. This provision is a legal principle which ensures that a company is legally bound by the acts of its employees providing those employees are acting within the ordinary course of their employment. The principle of 'strict liability' also applies to many environmental offences. This means that once the infringement can be proved to have been caused by the company then guilt is established even if a criminal intent cannot be proved.

(d) See above.

(e) See above.

2. The role of enforcing bodies and individuals in connection with environmental offences

(a) Environment Agency, Health & Safety Executive, sewerage undertakers, Local Authorities, Port/Harbour Authorities, English Nature/Countryside, Commission for Wales.

(b) Yes.

(c) Generally no, but in certain circumstances, e.g. water resources, prosecutions, either the Environment Agency itself or the Director of Public Prosecutions needs to give approval.

(d) The individual applies to a Court for a summons, which they must then serve on the alleged offender. That individual then appears at Court as the prosecutor. We regard this as an important safeguard for individuals should an organization fail to take appropriate action.

(e) —

(f) The Public Prosecutor in the UK (the Director of Public Prosecutions) does not undertake environmental offences. It is not the same in Scotland however, as the Prosecutor Fiscal acts as a Public prosecutor in all environmental offences.

(g) The enforcing bodies generally conduct the whole of the enquiry and subsequent prosecution.

(h) Enforcing bodies are the main regulator and thus contribute most Individual's role is a safeguard and extra watchdog.

3. Criminal penalties

(a) Imprisonment, community penalties, fine, discharge.

(b) Sanctions must commonly applied-fines. Waste offences average approximately £ 2,000 per offence with water offences being higher. The highest water pollution case so far is £750,000. Some prison sentences have been imposed, none longer than twelve months.

(c) Imprisonment is used rarely.

(d) We regard fines as generally low due to lack of familiarity by the Courts in dealing with environmental offending.

(e) All criminal sanctions are imposed by the Court.

4. Administrative Sanctions

(a) No, although scope for fixed penalties to be imposed for fishing offences. This provision in the Environment Act 1995 has, however, not been brought into force.

(b) Provision of a fixed penalty for an offence would be a criminal sanction.

(c) Civil sanctions in the form of injunctions are available. These can stop unlawful activity immediately so giving the enforcement body time to prepare a Court case. Enforcing Authorities also have power to revoke or vary environmental licences. These are not administrative sanctions as such but can ensure stricter regulatory control over operators. It can therefore be very effective.

(d) Administrative fines have not yet been introduced in the UK.

(f) Not applicable.

5. Existence of Instruments which Prohibit individuals from carrying out a similar activity

(a) Yes.

(b) Administrative tool which could lead to criminal sanction. The enforcing authority has powers to regulate operators under various legislative regimes depending on the media or type of process which is being regulated. The legislative regimes are primarily the Environmental Protection Act 1990 parts I and II (which regulate prescribed industries under an integrated pollution control regime) and Part II which regulates the waste disposal industry; the Water Resources Act 1991 which regulates discharges to water; the Radioactive Substances Act 1993 which regulated the use and disposal of radioactive waste and the Environment Act 1995 which established the Environment Agency as the principal environmental regulator in England and Wales. The enforcing authority can serve, under most regimes, prohibition, enforcement or works notices. Contravention of such notices can be an offence in its own right. The precise circumstances in which such notices are served, depends on the particular legislative regime. For instance, enforcement notices can be served under the Environmental Protection Act 1990 Part I Section 13 where the enforcing authority is of the opinion that the person carrying on the prescribed process under an authorization is contravening any condition of the authorization or is likely to contravene any such conditions. Prohibition notices can be served under Section 14 where the enforcing authority is of the opinion that the continuing to carry on a process, or the continuing to carry it on in a particular manner, involves an imminent risk of serious pollution of the environment. Under Section 21 Radioactive Substances Act 1993 enforcement notices can be served where a person is failing or likely to fail to comply with any condition or limit of the authorization, and prohibition notices under Section 22 where the continuing to carry on the activity involves an imminent risk of pollution of the environment or of harm to human health. Under Section 90B Water Resources Act 1991 enforcement notices can be served in similar circumstances, ie breach of conditions as improvement notices above. Under the Environmental Protection Act 1990 Part II Section 42 if a condition of a waste management licence is not being complied with, or is likely not to be, a notice may be served.

(c) Served by the enforcing body.

(d) See above.

(e) Approximately 400 notices are served each year.

(f) If this occurred then an injunction or prosecution would be initiated.

6. Transfrontier pollution incidents

(a) —

(b) —

(c) —

7. Criminal liability for environmental offences by public servants and public authorities

(a) Yes and no – Government Departments are immune but individuals are not. Local Authorities and the Environment Agency can similarly be liable.

(b) Additionally Central Government departments (Crown bodies) can face a Declaration in the High Court that their actions are unlawful.
Central Government, Local Authorities and the Environment Agency can also face civil claims in the High Court that they have acted in breach of statutory duty (a tort) or misfeasance in the carrying out of public duties. In addition, the UK has a very highly developed system of judicial review whereby individuals and companies can review the decisions of central Government, Local Authorities or the Environment Agency on procedural grounds. The High Court can force the administrative bodies to review or remake their decisions.

(c) In the same way as against any other offender.

(d) It is very rare that an individual, whoever they are, is held criminally liable.

8. Miscellaneous

(a) Injunctions are a speedy and effective administrative sanction, as yet are used only rarely.

(b) Large numbers of minor incidents only receive a warning as (hopefully) no environmental effect and it was a genuine mistake.

(c) There is a network of enforcing bodies which circulates its intelligence. Whether such information is of use evidentially or the enforcing body would wish to make application for it to be withheld would depend on its nature.

EXAMPLES OF ENFORCEMENT NOTICES

(i) University College, London

An enforcement notice was served on University College, London under RSA 93. The University carried out teaching and research involving the disposal of radioactive waste and has a certificate of authorization under RSA 93.

During a routine inspection of the University it was found that they were not complying with one of the conditions in their certificate of authorization, and that adequate records were not being kept so as to demonstrate compliance with the limits on the certificate.

There were over 20 departments disposing of radioactive waste within the University in Central London, but there was no system in place to ensure that the authorized limits were complied with.

The enforcement notice, served on 7 November, required the University, by 8 December, to:

> 'ensure that each department within the University makes a return showing the monthly disposal;
>
> keep records of all disposals of radioactive waste in a format so as to demonstrate compliance with the monthly limit set out in the authorization.'

(ii) GH Besseler Associates CRU Limited, Hyde Street, Leeds

Enforcement notices were served on the above company under RSA 93. The company carries out clinical research and new pharmaceuticals.

The action followed a site inspection which revealed a number of deficiencies in the manner in which radioactive material intended for use in clinical research was kept, and also identified inadequate procedures for the handling and storing of the resultant waste.

In particular,

(i) holdings of the registered material were in excess of the registered limit of 25 megabequerels of radioactivity;
(ii) neither the material store nor the waste store were clearly identified;
(iii) procedures did not fully address the requirements to ensure full compliance with the certificate.

The notices required the company to act within 4 days to remedy the more immediate problems covering storage and identification and required a revised application to be made for the keeping and use of the material. Within 2 months the company was required to have reviewed and implemented procedures for:

(i) keeping radioactive materials;
(ii) minimising, where practical, waste produced during its use; and
(iii) specifying systems for accumulation and disposal of the waste.

The radioactive material consisted of small amounts of low level radio isotopes, held in liquid form in a pharmacy at the site. After use, the waste produced was stored on the premises, prior to disposal by incineration elsewhere.

The potential hazard from the radioactive material was considered to be low. It would have to be ingested to have any impact.

The action was taken to ensure that proper safeguards for the keeping, use and disposal of all radioactive materials were adhered to.

EXAMPLE OF PROHIBITION NOTICE

University of Aston, Birmingham

A prohibition notice was served against the University of Aston, Birmingham, who are registered and authorized under RSA 93 to keep and use radioactive materials and dispose of radioactive wastes generated from teaching and research activities.

Following a visit, and subsequent investigation, a number of failings had been identified in the University's procedures for recording receipt of radioactive materials, for the subsequent handling of this material and for the final disposal of waste generated.

Due to the risk of environmental harm resulting from these failings, a prohibition notice was served on the University on 15 December 1995. This notice required the University to immediately cease generating and disposing of radioactive waste until a current inventory of radioactive materials and wastes was established to enable disposal of waste to occur in accordance with the authorization.

EXAMPLES OF PROSECUTION

(i) CET Flexitech Limited

This company was successfully prosecuted for breach of RSA 93 in respect of failure to comply with registration conditions relating to the storage of radioactive sources at its premises in Kent.

The company had a certificate of registration, issued under RSA 1960, to use radioactive sources for moisture and density measurement at premises in England and Wales.During the course of a routine inspection, the door to the radioactive source store was found to have been left open. Gauges containing radioactive sources were being kept in the store at the time and were unattended. The store is readily accessible from a nearby public road.

The company pleaded guilty to an offence under the Act and was fined £7,000. Costs of £2,500 were awarded against the company.

(ii) I G E Medical Systems, St Albans

I G E Medical Systems, St Albans were successfully prosecuted, over the loss of a closed radioactive source. The company had re-written the local rules for logging the movements of some of the sources it held, without informing HMIP. This resulted in a significant relaxation of control of the sources. The source was lost some time during a 3 month period but the exact date could not be established. The site was being closed down with the loss of 200 jobs during the period during which the source went missing. Strenuous efforts, including contacting all past employees, were made to recover the source but were not successful. It is likely that the source was sent to a landfill site. The company pleaded guilty and was fined £5,000 with £5,754.75 costs.

(iii) Nissan Motor Manufacturing UK, Sunderland

This company was prosecuted for breach over RSA 93 for the loss of a polonium 210 radioactive source from its Sunderland site some time between 27 and 29 January 1995.

The source was used as a process control device in paint spraying operations.

The company pleaded guilty of failing to prevent the loss of the source and was fined £10,000. Costs of £5,220 were also awarded against the company

Over the period 1990 to 1995, HMIP brought 19 prosecutions for contravention of the requirements of RSA 93.

DEFENDANT	FUNCTION	COURT & DATE	FINE	COSTS AWARDED	LEGAL COSTS
British Nuclear Fuels Plc	IPC/RAS	Whitehaven MC 04–04–97	£20,000	£3,844.08	£3,240
John Lee	Waste	Crewe MC 22.04.97	£1,000	£610	£370
Robinson Brothers (Disposal Services) Ltd	Waste	Bootle MC 29.04.97	£10,000	£900	
GATX Terminals Ltd	Water Quality	Wallasey MC 14.05.97	£2,000	£2,368.98	
Gary Chadwick t/a Wigan Crushing Services	Water Quality	Chorley MC 21.05.97	£3,000	£498.50	£445
W Hargreaves Ltd	Water Quality	Blackburn MC 23.09.97	£3,000	£1,437.29	£445
Richard Brewood	Waste	Macclesfield MC 02.05.97	£100	£140	
Stephen G Hilton	Waste	Preston CC 19.05.97	£1,500	£4,000	
Jason Lang	Waste	Salford MC 08.05.97	2 year Con Dis	£90	
Darren Holloway	Waste	Salford MC 08.05.97	2 year Con Dis	£90	
Ind Coope Oxford & West Ltd	Water Quality	Southport MC 04.06.97	£2,000	£1,274.91	£900
Tarmac Heavy Building Materials Ltd	Water Quality	Carlisle MC 12.06.97	£2,500	£598	£550

Continued

DEFENDANT	FUNCTION	COURT & DATE	FINE	COSTS AWARDED	LEGAL COSTS
David Stubbs and John Stubbs	Water Quality	Vale Royal MC 10.06.97	2 year Con Dis 2 year Con Dis	£588 £588	£350
Adrian Wade	Waste	Bootle MC 18.06.97	£500	£450	
Lanstar Ltd	Waste	Warrington CC 30.06.97	£24,000	£8,517	
Shafique Ali	Water Quality	Reedley MC 31.07.97	£100	£150	£150 (£900)
ICI Chemicals & Polymers Ltd	IPC/RAS	Widnes MC 02.07.97	£34,000	£6,000	£1,500
P J Whitter	Waste	Preston CC 11.07.97	£5,000	£1,500	
R McBrides Ltd	Water Quality	Rochdale MC 06.08.97	£7,500	£687.85	£547.50
Norfrost Haulage Ltd	Water Quality	Leyland MC 11.08.97	£12,000	£343,80	£315
Huntapac Produce Ltd	Water Quality	Ormskirk MC 11.08.97	£8,000	£864.67	£480
Huntapac Produce Ltd	Water Quality	Ormskirk MC 11.08.97	£12,000	£607.74	£375
Mrs. Hanbury	Water Quality	Carlisle MC 12.08.97	£2,000	£3,500	£3,182.90
Statestrong Ltd	Water Quality	Lytham MC 12.08.97	£5,000	£416	£370

Continued

DEFENDANT	FUNCTION	COURT & DATE	FINE	COSTS AWARDED	LEGAL COSTS
Trichem North Ltd	Water Quality	South Ribble Mc 18.08.97	£3,000	£1,650.31	£480
North County Foods Ltd	Water Quality	W. Allerdale MC 20.08.97	£4,000	£978.39	£660
B Wardle & Co t/a Wardle Storeys	Waste	Reedley MC 07.08.97	£16,000	£2,299.50	£1,372.50
Vale Royal BC	Waste	Northwich MC 19.08.97	£4,000	£678	
Mark Abel	Water Resources	Crewe MC 26.08.97	£2,000	£1,170.30	£520
Lakeland Foods Ltd	Water Quality	Kendal MC 08.09.97	£2,000	£384.56	£384.56
George Whitelock	Waste	Liverpool CC 8–12.09.97	3 months imprisonment	None awarded	
Spotmix Ltd	Waste	Bootle MC 23.09.97	£8,000	£2,182.22	£1,590
British Nuclear Fuels Plc	IPC/RAS Water Quality	Whitehaven MC 26.09.97	£32,500	£24,954.77	£3,900
West Coast Corrygated Ltd	Water Quality	Knowsley MC 03.10.97	£1,000	£349.56	£349.56
1. Autobar Ltd 2. P&H (1925) Ltd	Water Quality	St. Helens MC 07.10.97	1. £3,000 2. £3,000	Cost to be determined	

Continued

DEFENDANT	FUNCTION	COURT & DATE	FINE	COSTS AWARDED	LEGAL COSTS
Vickers Shipbuilding & Engineering Ltd	Water Quality	Barrow MC 10.10.97	£12,000	£3,522.15	£1,998
1. M Bell	Water Quality	Carlisle MC 14.10.97	1. £2,500 2. £2,500	1. £216.02 2. £216,02	£432.04
J. Barker	Water Quality	Hyndburn MC 20.10.97	2 months imprisonment	None awarded	
Castle Cement	IPC/RAS	Blackburn MC 17.10.97	£2,000 £2,000 £2,000 £500	£2,000	
P Miller	Waste	Rawtenstall MC 02.10.97	Absolute Discharge	£150	£150
1. Hassal Homes Ltd 2. T Armstrong 3. I Milbourn	Waste	Carlisle MC 02.10.97	1. £3,000 no sep. penalty 2. £1,000 3. £500	1. £1,000 2. £332 3. £100	
RN Holt	Waste	Rossendale MC 23.10.97	3 × 2 year Con.Disch	£1,640	£640
Greenwood Environmental Ltd	Waste	Preston MC 29.10.97	£5,000	£1,324	
	TOTALS	£266,700	£85,212.62	£25,697.06	

The RAS function is about to develop its functional prosecution strategy.

Brief Information on the system of investigation and criminal prosecution of suspected environmental crimes (Structure of the national legal prosecution system)

England and Wales

The environment agency is the responsible body for investigating environmental offences in England and Wales. The agency may cooperate with other enforcement bodies, including the police, when investigating offences. The agency also liaises with health and safety officials, environmental health officers and local council personnel. Environmental offences are statutory and are crimes and will only be dealt with by the Criminal Court. The same system for criminal proceedings apply whatever the type of offence, whether it be pollution of a water course or a murder. The Environment Agency does not have the exclusive right to prosecute environmental crime. An individual also has the right to bring a private prosecution.

Scotland

Criminal proceedings are conducted by a public prosecutor known as the Procurator Fiscal (or the Lord Advocate in the most serious cases), who determines whether it is in the public interest to commence such proceedings. Private prosecution by an individual does exist as a concept, but from the practical point of view should be ignored due to its extreme rarity. SEPA has the status of a 'non-police reporting agency' with primary responsibility for investigation apparent environmental criminal conduct and reporting it (including all necessary evidence) to the Procurator Fiscal. SEPA may cooperate with other enforcement bodies, including the police, when investigating offences. SEPA also liaises with health and safety officials, environmental health officers and local authority personnel. Environmental offences are statutory and are crimes and will only be dealt with by the criminal court. The same system for criminal proceedings applies whatever the type of offence, whether it be pollution of a water course or a murder. SEPA does not have exclusive responsibility to report environmental crime to the Procurator Fiscal Service.

ANNEX 3: CONVENTION ON THE PROTECTION OF THE ENVIRONMENT THROUGH CRIMINAL LAW[1]

Preamble

The Member States of the Council of Europe and the other States signatory hereto,

Considering that the aim of the Council of Europe is to achieve a greater unity between its members;

Convinced of the need to pursue a common criminal policy aimed at the protection of the environment;

Considering that unregulated industrial development may give rise to a degree of pollution which poses risks to the environment;

Considering that life and health of human beings, the environmental media and fauna and flora must be protected by all possible means;

Considering that the uncontrolled use of technology and the excessive exploitation of natural resources ental serious environmental hazards which must be overzome by appropriate and concerted measures;

---

1 Council of Europe, ETS No. 172, published on the internet: <http://www.coe.fr/eng/legaltxt/172e.htm.> An earlier version of this Convention is publies in *Van den Wijngaert/Stessens* (Eds.), International Criminal Law. A Collection of International and European Instruments, 134–141.

Recognising that, whilst the prevention of the impairment of the environment must be achieved primarily thourgh other measures, criminal law has an important part to play in protecting the environment;

Recalling that environmental violations having serious consequences must be established as criminal offences subject to appropriate sanctions;

Wishing to take effective measures to ensure that the perpetrators of such acts do not escape prosecution and punishment and desirous of fostering international co-operation to this end;

Convinced that imposing criminal or administrative sanctions on legal persons can play an effective role in the prevntion of environmental violations and noting the growing international trend in this regard;

Mindful of the existing interntional conventions which already contain provisions aiming at the protection of the environment through criminal law;

Having regard to the conclusions of the 7th and 17th Conferences of European Ministers of Justice held in Basle in 1972 and in Istanbul in 1990, and to Recommendations 1192 (1992) of the Parliamentary Assembly,

Have agreed as follows:

Section 1 – Use of Terms

Article 1 – Definitions

For the purposes of this Convention:

(a) 'unlawful' means infringing a law, an administrative regulation or a decision taken by a competent authority, aiming at the protection of the environment;
(b) 'water' means groundwater and surface water including the water of lakes, rivers, oceans and seas.

Section II – Measures to be taken at a National Level

Article 2 – Intentional offences

1. Each Party shall adopt such appropriate measures as may be necessary to establish as criminal offences under its domestic law:
   (a) the discharge, emission or introduction of a quantity of substances or ionising radiation into air, soil or water, which:
      (i) causes death or serious injury to any person, or
      (ii) creates a significant risk of causing death or serious injury to any person;
   (b) the unlawful discharge, emission or introduction of a quantity of substances or ionising radiation into air, soil or water, which causes or is likely to cause their

lasting deterioration or death or serious injury to any person or substantial damage to protected monuments, other protected objects, property, animals or plants;

(c) the unlawful disposal, treatment, storage, transport, export or import of hazardous waste, which causes or is likely to cause death or serious injury to any person or substantial damage to the quality of air, soil, water, animals or plants;

(d) the unlawful operation of a plant in which a dangerous activity is carried out and which causes or is likely to cause death or serious injury to any person or substantial damage to the quality of air, soil, water, animals or plants;

(e) the unlawful manufacture, treatment, storage, use, transport, export or import of nuclear materials or other hazardous radioactive substances which causes or is likely to cause death or serious injury to any person or substantial damage to the quality of air, soil, water, animals or plants,

when committed intentionally.

2. Each Party shall adopt such appropriate measures as may be necessary to establish as criminal offences under its domestic law aiding or abetting the commission of any of the offences established in accordance with paragraph 1 of this Article.

Article 3 – Negligent offences

1. Each Party shall adopt such appropriate measures as may be necessary to establish as criminal offences under its domestic law, when committed with negligence, the offences enumerated in Article 2, subparagraph 1 a – e.
2. Any State, at the time of signature or when depositing its instrument of ratification, acceptance, approval or accession, by a declaration addressed to the Secretary General of the Council of Europe, declare that paragraph 1 of this article, in part or in whole, shall only apply to offences which were committed with gross negligence.
3. Any State may, at the time of signature or when depositing its instrument of ratification, acceptance, approval or accession, by a declaration addressed to the Secretary General of the Council of Europe, declare that paragraph 1 of this Article, in part or in whole, shall not apply to:
   - subparagraph 1 a. ii of Article 2
   - subparagraph 1 b of Article 2, insofar as the offence relates to protected monuments, to other protected objects or to property.

Article 4 – Other Criminal Offences or Administrative Offences

Insofar as these are not covered by the provisions of Articles 2 and 3, each Party shall adopt such appropriate measures as may be necessary to establish as criminal offences or administrative offences, liable to sanctions or other measures under its domestic law, when committed intentionally or with negligence:

(a) the unlawful discharge, emission or introduction of a quantity of substances or ionising radiation into air, soil or water;

(b) the unlawful causing of noise;

(c) the unlawful disposal, treatment, storage, transport, export or import of waste;
(d) the unlawful operation of a plant;
(e) the unlawful manufacture, treatment, use, transport, export or import of nuclear materials, other radioactive substances or hazardous chemicals;
(f) the unlawful causing of changes detrimental to natural components of a national park, nature reserve, water conservation area or other protected areas;
(g) the unlawful possession, taking, damaging, killing or trading of or in protected wild flora and fauna species.

Article 5 – Jurisdiction

1. Each Party shall adopt such appropriate measures as may be necessary to establish jurisdiction over a criminal offence established in accordance with this Convention when the offence is committed:
   (a) in its territory; or
   (b) on board a ship or an aircraft registered in it or flying its flag; or
   (c) by one of its nationals if the offence is punishable under criminal law where it was committed or if the place where it was committed does not fall under any territorial jurisdiction.
2. Each Party shall adopt such appropriate measures as may be necessary to establish jurisdiction over a criminal offence established in accordance with this Convention, in cases where an alleged offender is present in its territory and it does not extradite him to another Party after a request for extradition.
3. This Convention does not exclude any criminal jurisdiction exercised by a Party in accordance with its domestic law.
4. Each Party may, at the time of signature or when depositing its instrument of ratification, acceptance, approval or accession, by a declaration addressed to the Secretary General of the Council of Europe, declare that paragraphs 1 and 2 of this article, in part or in whole, shall not apply.

Article 6 – Sanctions for environmental offences

Each Party shall adopt, in accordance with the relevant international instruments, such appropriate measures as may be necessary to enable it to make the offences established in accordance with Articles 2 and 3 punishable by criminal sanctions which take into account the serious nature of these offences. The sanctions available shall include imprisonment and pecuniary sanctions and may include reinstatement of the environment.

Article 7 – Confiscation measures

1. Each Party shall adopt such appropriate measures as may be necessary to enable it to confiscate instrumentalities and proceeds, or property the value of which corresponds to such proceeds, in respect of offences enumerated in Articles 2 and 3.

2. Each Party may, at the time of signature or when depositing its instrument of ratification, acceptance, approval or accession, by a declaration addressed to the Secretary General of the Council of Europe, declare that it will not apply paragraph 1 of this Article either in respect of offences specified in such declaration or in respect of certain categories or instrumentalities or of proceeds, or property the value of which corresponds to such proceeds.

Article 8 – Reinstatement of the environment

Each Party may, at any time, in a declaration addressed to the Secretary General of the Council of Europe, declare that it will provide for reinstatement of the environment according to the following provisions of this article:

(a) the competent authority may order the reinstatement of the environment in relation to an offence established in accordance with this Convention. Such an order may be made subject to certain conditions;
(b) where an order for the reinstatement of the environment has not been complied with, the competent authority may, in accordance with domestic law, make it executable at the expense of the person subject to the order or that person may be liable to other criminal sanctions instead of or in addition to it.

Article 9 – Corporate liability

1. Each Party shall adopt such appropriate measures as may be necessary to enable it to impose criminal or administrative sanctions or measures on legal persons on whose behalf an offence referred to in Articles 2 or 3 has been committed by their organs, or by members thereof or by another representative.
2. Corporate liability under paragraph 1 of this article shall not exclude criminal proceedings against a natural person.
3. Any State may, at the time of signature or when depositing its instrument of ratification, acceptance, approval or accession, by a declaration addressed to the Secretary General of the Council of Europe, declare that it reserves the right not to apply paragraph 1 of this article or any part thereof or that it applies only to offences specified in such declaration.

Article 10 – Co-operation between authorities

1. Each Party shall adopt such appropriate measures as may be necessary to ensure that the authorities responsible for environmental protection cooperate with the authorities responsible for investigating and prosecuting criminal offences:
   (a) by informing the latter authorities, on their own initiative, where there are reasonable grounds to believe that an offence under Article 2 has been committed;
   (b) by providing, upon request, all necessary information to the latter authorities, in accordance with domestic law.

2. Any State may, at the time of signature or when depositing its instrument of ratification, acceptance, approval or accession, by a declaration addressed to the Secretary General of the Council of Europe, declare that it reserves the right not to apply paragraph 1a. of this Article or that it applies only to offences specified in such declaration.

Article 11 – Rights for groups to participate in proceedings

Each Party may, at any time, in a declaration, addressed to the Secretary General of the Council of Europe, declare that it will, in accordance with domestic law, grant any group, foundation or association which, according to its statutes, aims at the protection of the environment, the right to participate in criminal proceedings concerning offences established in accordance with this Convention.

Section III – Measures to be taken at international level

Article 12 – International co-operation

1. The Parties shall afford each other, in accordance with the provisions of relevant international instruments on international co-operation in criminal matters and with their domestic law, the widest measure of co-operation in investigations and judicial proceedings relating to criminal offences established in accordance with this Convention.
2. The Parties may afford each other assistance in investigations and proceedings relating to those acts defined in Article 4 of this Convention which are not covered by paragraph 1 of this article.

Section IV – Final Clauses

Article 13 – Signature and entry into force

1. This Convention shall be open for signature by the member States of the Council of Europe and non-member States which have participated in its elaboration. Such States may express their consent to be bound by:
   (a) signature without reservation as to ratification, acceptance or approval; or
   (b) signature subject to ratification, acceptance or approval, followed by ratification, acceptance or approval.
2. Instruments of ratification, acceptance or approval shall be deposited with the Secretary General of the Council of Europe.
3. This Convention shall enter into force on the first day of the month following the expiration of a period of three months after the date on which three States have expressed their consent to be bound by the Convention in accordance with the provisions of paragraph 1.
4. In respect of any signatory State which subsequently expresses its consent to be bound by it, the Convention shall enter into force on the first day of the month

following the expiration of a period of three months after the date of the expression of its consent to be bound by the Convention in accordance with the provisions of paragraph 1.

Article 14 – Accession to the Convention

1. After the entry into force of this Convention, the Committee of Ministers of the Council of Europe, after consulting the Contracting States to the Convention, may invite any State not a member of the Council of Europe to accede to this Convention, by a decision taken by the majority provided for in Article 20.d of the Statute of the Council of Europe and by the unanimous vote of the representatives of the Contracting States entitled to sit on the Committee.
2. In respect of any acceding State, the Convention shall enter into force on the first day of the month following the expiration of a period of three months after the date of deposit of the instrument of accession with the Secretary General of the Council of Europe.

Article 15 – Territorial application

1. Any State may, at the time of signature or when depositing its instrument of ratification, acceptance, approval or accession, specify the territory or territories to which this Convention shall apply.
2. Any State may, at any later date, by a declaration addressed to the Secretary General of the Council of Europe, extend the application of this Convention to any other territory specified in the declaration. In respect of such territory the Convention shall enter into force on the first day of the month following the expiration of a period of three months after the date of receipt of such declaration by the Secretary General.
3. Any declaration made under the two preceding paragraphs may, in respect of any territory specified in such declaration, be withdrawn by a notification addressed to the Secretary General. The withdrawal shall become effective on the first day of the month following the expiration of a period of three months after the date of receipt of such notification by the Secretary General.

Article 16 – Relationship with other conventions and agreements

1. This Convention does not affect the rights and undertakings derived from international multilateral conventions concerning special matters.
2. The Parties to the Convention may conclude bilateral or multilateral agreements with one another on the matters dealt with in this Convention, for purposes of supplementing or strengthening its provisions or facilitating the application of the principles embodied in it.
3. If two or more Parties have already concluded an agreement or treaty in respect of a subject which is dealt with in this Convention or otherwise have established their relations in respect of that subject, they shall be entitled to apply that agreement or

treaty or to regulate those relations accordingly, in lieu of the present Convention, if it facilitates international co-operation.

Article 17 – Reservations

1. Any State may, at the time of signature or when depositing its instrument of ratification, acceptance, approval or accession, declare that it avails itself of one or more of the reservations provided for in Article 3, paragraphs 2 and 3, Article 5, paragraph 4, Article 7, paragraph 2, Article 9, paragraph 3 and Article 10, paragraph 2. No other reservation may be made.
2. Any State which has made a reservation under the preceding paragraph may wholly or partly withdraw it by means of a notification addressed to the Secretary General of the Council of Europe. The withdrawal shall take effect on the date of receipt of such notification by the Secretary General.
3. A Party which has made a reservation in respect of a provision of this Convention may not claim the application of that provision by any other Party; it may, however, if its reservation is partial or conditional, claim the application of that provision in so far as it has itself accepted it.

Article 18 – Amendments

1. Amendments to this Convention may be proposed by any Party, and shall be communicated by the Secretary General of the Council of Europe to the member States of the Council of Europe and to every non-member State which has acceded to or has been invited to accede to this Convention in accordance with the provisions of Article 14.
2. Any amendment proposed by a Party shall be communicated to the European Committee on Crime Problems which shall submit to the Committee of Ministers its opinion on that proposed amendment.
3. The Committee of Ministers shall consider the proposed amendment and the opinion submitted by the European Committee on Crime Problems and may adopt the amendment.
4. The text of any amendment adopted by the Committee of Ministers in accordance with paragraph 3 of this article shall be forwarded to the Parties for acceptance.
5. Any amendment adopted in accordance with paragraph 3 of this article shall come into force on the thirtieth day after all Parties have informed the Secretary General of their acceptance thereof.

Article 19 – Settlement of disputes

1. The European Committee on Crime Problems of the Council of Europe shall be kept informed regarding the interpretation and application of this Convention.
2. In case of a dispute between Parties as to the interpretation or application of this Convention, they shall seek a settlement of the dispute through negotiation or any other peaceful means of their choice, including submission of the dispute to the

European Committee on Crime Problems, to an arbitral tribunal whose decisions shall be binding upon the Parties, or to the International Court of Justice, as agreed upon by the Parties concerned.

Article 20 – Denunciation

1. Any Party may, at any time, denounce this Convention by means of a notification addressed to the Secretary General of the Council of Europe.
2. Such denunciation shall become effective on the first day of the month following the expiration of a period of three months after the date of receipt of the notification by the Secretary General.

Article 21 – Notifications

The Secretary General of the Council of Europe shall notify the member States of the Council of Europe and any State which has acceded to this Convention of:

(a) any signature;
(b) the deposit of any instrument of ratification, acceptance, approval or accession;
(c) any date of entry into force of this Convention in accordance with Articles 13 and 14;
(d) any reservation made under Article 17, paragraph 1;
(e) any other act, notification or communication relating to this Convention.
In witness whereof the undersigned, being duly authorised thereto, have signed this Convention.

Done at Strasbourg, the 4th day of November 1998, in English and in French, both texts being equally authentic, in a single copy which shall be deposited in the archives of the Council of Europe. The Secretary General of the Council of Europe shall transmit certified copies to each member State of the Council of Europe and to any State invited to accede to it.

ANNEX 4: RESOLUTIONS OF THE XVTH INTERNATIONAL CONGRESS OF PENAL LAW (RIO DE JANEIRO, SEPTEMBER 4th–10th 1994)

RESOLUTIONS

SECTION I:

CRIMES AGAINST THE ENVIRONMENT. APPLICATION OF THE GENERAL PART

SECTION II:

COMPUTER CRIMES AND OTHER CRIMES AGAINST INFORMATION TECHNOLOGY

SECTION III:

REFORM MOVEMENTS IN CRIMINAL PROCEDURE AND THE PROTECTION OF HUMAN RIGHTS

SECTION IV:

THE REGIONALIZATION OF INTERNATIONAL CRIMINAL LAW AND THE PROTECTION OF HUMAN RIGHTS IN INTERNATIONAL COOPERATIVE PROCEDURES IN CRIMINAL MATTERS

RESOLUTION ON THE INTERNATIONAL CRIMINAL COURT

SECTION I

CRIMES AGAINST THE ENVIRONMENT

APPLICATION OF THE GENERAL PART

PREAMBLE

Considering the increasing risks to the present and future generations, their health, and the environment of which they are a part, posed by industrial and similar activities;

Considering worldwide concerns about the degradation of the environment caused, *inter alia* by the commission of crimes against the environment contrary to national and international laws;

Considering recent developments towards the recognition of crimes against the environment in national penal codes and environmental protection laws and in international conventions, recommendations and resolutions;

Considering the Council of Europe Resolution 77(28) on the *Contribution of Criminal Law to the Protection of the Environment*, Recommendation 88(18) on the *Liability of Enterprises for Offences*, Resolution No. 1 of the European Ministers of Justice adopted at their Conference in Istanbul in 1990 and the on-going work of the Council of Europe towards the development of a European Convention on the protection of the environment through criminal law;

Considering the United Nations General Assembly Resolution No. 45/121 of 1990 adopting the Resolution on the protection of the environment through criminal law submitted by the Eighth UN Congress on the Prevention of Crime and the Treatment of Offenders; the United Nations Economic and Social Council Resolution 1993/32 and June 1994 and the preparatory documents of the forthcoming Ninth UN Congress on the Prevention of Crime and the Treatment of Offenders on agenda item *'Action against national and transnational economic and organized crime and the role of criminal law in the protection of the environment'*;

Considering the recommendations contained in the report of the International Law Commission to the UN General Assembly, 1991;

Considering the *Model for a domestic law of crimes against the environment* proposed by an International meeting of experts on environmental crime held in Portland, Oregon from 19–23 March 1994;

Considering the desirability of providing appropriate sanctions for serious crimes against the environment and for the reparation of damage to the environment;

Having examined and deliberated upon the recommendations of the AIDP Preparatory Colloquium on the application of criminal law to crimes against the environment held in Ottawa, Canada from 2–6 November 1992,

RECOMMENDATIONS

I. GENERAL PRINCIPLES

1. Environment means all components of the earth, both abiotic and biotic, and includes air and all layers of the atmosphere, water, land, including soil and mineral resources, flora and fauna, and all ecological inter-relations among these components.

2. The *Principle of Sustainable Development*, as articulated by the World Commission on Environment and Development in 1986 (better known as the Brundtland Commission) and adopted by the General Assembly of the United Nations in 1992, states that economic development to meet the needs of the present generation should not compromise the ability of future generations to meet their own needs.

3. The *Precautionary Principle*, as articulated by the United Nations Conference on Environment and Development held in Rio de Janeiro in June 1992 and adopted by the General Assembly of the United Nations, states that where there are threats of serious or irreversible damage, lack of full scientific certainty shall not be used as a reason for postponing cost-effective measures to prevent environmental degradation.

4. States and society have a responsibility to ensure as far as possible that the Principle of Sustainable Development and the Precautionary Principle are respected by all natural persons and private and public entities involved in activities that have the potential to harm the environment.

5. To ensure the observance of the Principle of Sustainable Development and the Precautionary Principle, States must have available a wide range of compliance measures including compliance incentives, enforceable compliance agreements, licensing and regulatory powers, and sanctions for failure to observe established standards. In appropriate cases, criminal law might be seen as providing cost-effective measures to ensure the protection of the environment.

II. SPECIFIC ISSUES IN RELATION TO CRIMES AGAINST THE ENVIRONMENT

6. Consistent with the principle of legality, there should be certainty in the definition of crimes against the environment.

7. A distinction should be drawn between sanctions which are imposed for non-observance of established administrative and regulatory standards, which do not include deprivation of liberty or punitive closing of an enterprise, and criminal sanctions which are imposed to prevent and punish culpable acts or omissions that cause serious harm to the environment.

8. The minimum material element in offences against the environment subject to criminal sanctions should be:

(a) an act or omission that causes serious harm to the environment or to human beings; or
(b) an act or omission in contravention of established environmental standards that creates a real and imminent (concrete) endangerment to the environment or human beings.

9. The minimum mental element, with respect both to an act or omission and to its consequences, required in the definition of an offence against the environment subject to criminal sanctions should be knowledge, intent, recklessness (*dolus eventualis or culpa gravis* or its equivalent in national laws) or, in cases where serious consequences are in issue, culpable negligence.

10. Where it is established that an accused acted or omitted to act, knowing that serious harm to the environment would likely result, and such harm does in fact result compliance with the terms of a licence or permit or with standards and prescriptions laid down in regulations should be reasonably limited as a justification for the act or omission.

11. Consistent with the *principle of restraint*, criminal sanctions should be utilized only when civil and administrative sanctions and remedies are inappropriate or ineffective to deal with particular offences against the environment.

III. CRIMINAL LIABILITY OF ENTITIES

12. Conduct that merits imposition of criminal sanctions can be engaged in by private and public entities as well as by natural persons.

13. National legal systems should, wherever possible under their constitution or basic law, provide for a variety of criminal sanctions and/or other measures adapted to private and public entities.

14. Where a private or a public entity is engaged in an activity that poses a serious risk of harm to the environment or to human beings, the managers and directing authorities of such entity should be required to exercise supervisory responsibility in a manner to prevent occurrence of harm and the entity should be held criminally liable if serious harm results as a consequence of the failure of its managers and directing authorities to properly discharge this supervisory responsibility.

15. To minimize the risk of injustice arising from uneven application of laws concerning offences against the environment in different countries, domestic laws should specify as clearly as possible the criteria establishing liability of human agents within private or public entities who may be responsible for ensuring compliance with environmental laws for offences against the environment committed by such entities.

PRIVATE ENTITIES

16. Where allowed under the constitution or the basic law of a country, notwithstanding the usual requirement of personal responsibility for criminal offences, proceedings against a private entity should be possible for offences against the environment even if responsibility for such offences cannot be directly attributed to any identified human agent of such entity.

17. Where a private entity is responsible for serious harm to the environment or human beings, proceedings against such entity should be possible for offences against the environment, regardless of whether the harm results from an individual act and/or omission or from cumulative acts and/or omissions over time.

18. Imposition of criminal sanctions or other measures against a private entity should not exonerate culpable human agents of such entity who are involved in the commission of offences against the environment.

PUBLIC ENTITIES

19. Where a public entity, in the course of executing its public functions or otherwise, causes serious harm to the environment or to human beings or, in contravention of established environmental standards, creates a real and imminent (*concrete*) endangerment to the environment or human beings, it should be possible to prosecute the criminally responsible human agents of such entity for an offence against the environment.

20. Where it is possible under the constitution or basic law of a country to hold a public entity responsible for criminal offences committed in the course

of executing its public functions or otherwise, proceedings against such entity should be possible for crimes against the environment even if responsibility for the crime cannot be directly attributed to any identified human agent of such entity.

IV. CRIMES AGAINST THE ENVIRONMENT

21. Core crimes against the environment, that is crimes that are *sui generis* and do not depend on other laws for their content, should be specified in national penal codes.

22. Where offences against the environment are subject to criminal sanctions, their key elements should be specified in legislation and not left to be determined by subordinate delegated authorities.

23. Core crimes against the environment affecting more than one national jurisdiction or affecting the global commons outside any national jurisdiction should be recognized as international crimes under multilateral conventions.

24. Within the framework of the constitution and the basic law of national legal systems, legislation should facilitate the participation of citizens in the initiation of investigation and prosecution of alleged crimes against the environment.

V. JURISDICTION

TRANS-BORDER CRIMES

25. Where the harm or serious risk of harm (*concrete endangerment*) that underlies a core crime against the environment arises outside the jurisdiction of a State where the crime is committed, wholly or in part, it should be possible, subject to appropriate safeguards for the accused and to applicable international laws, to prosecute the accused in the State where the crime was committed or in any State where the harm or serious risk of harm arises.

EXTRA-TERRITORIAL CRIMES

26. Where the harm or serious risk of harm (*concrete endangerment*) that underlies a core crime against the environment arises in the global commons, States should agree on an international convention or implement existing international conventions that would enable them to prosecute the crime by applying, in the following order: the flag principle; the principle of nationality; the principle of *extradite or prosecute*; and, in cases of generally acknowledged international crimes, the principle of universality.

EXTRADITION

27. Crimes against the environment of particularly serious gravity should be made extraditable offences.

INTERNATIONAL CRIMINAL COURT

28. In order to facilitate the prosecution of international crimes, in particular crimes against the global commons, the jurisdiction of the international court proposed by the International Law Commission and currently being considered by the General Assembly of the United Nations should include crimes against the global commons.

IMPLEMENTATION OF INTERNATIONAL CONVENTIONS

29. Where international conventions respecting crimes against the environment are not self-executing under domestic law with respect to execution of criminal sanctions, signatory States should implement such conventions by enacting the necessary domestic legislation.

COMPARATIVE ENVIRONMENTAL LAW AND POLICY SERIES

1. Environmental Contracts – Comparative Approaches to Regulatory Innovation in the United States and Europe, Eric W. Orts and Kurt Deketelaere (eds.). ISBN 90-411-9821-0
2. Environmental Regulation through Financial Organisations – Comparative Perspectives on the Industrialised Nations, Benjamin J. Richardson (ed.). ISBN 90-411-1735-0
3. Access to Justice in Environmental Matters in the EU/Accés à la justice en matiére d'environnement dans l'UE, Jonas Ebbesson (ed.). ISBN 90-411-1826-8
4. Civil Liability for Environmental Damage – A Comparative Analysis of Law and Policy in Europe and the United States, Mark Wilde (ed.). ISBN 90-411-1891-8
5. Public Environmental Law in the European Union and the United States – A Comparative Analysis, René J.G.H. Seerden, Michiel A. Heldeweg and Kurt R. Deketelaere (eds.). ISBN 90-411-1926-4
6. International, EC and US Environmental Law – A Comparative Selection of Basic Documents, Kurt Deketelaere and Jan Gekiere (eds.). ISBN 90-411-1938-8
7. Public Interest Environmental Litigation in India, Pakistan and Bangladesh, Jona Razzaque (ed.). ISBN 90-411-2214-1
8. Criminal Enforcement of Environmental Law in the European Union, Michael Faure and Günter Heine (eds.). ISBN 90-411-2337-7
9. Legal Remedies for Marine Pollution, Michael Faure (ed.). ISBN 90-411-2338-5